Y0-BDJ-860

Copyright © Blue Apron, Inc.

Blue Apron team: Leila Clifford, Jared Cluff, TJ DiFrancesco, Winnie Jeng, Lucas Kalina, Timothy F. Kemp, Claire King, James Molloy, Chris Montgomery, Mandi O'Brien, Ilia Papas, Judith Peña, Matt Salzberg, Christopher M. Sorensen, Matthew Wadiak, Melissa Warren and Rani Yadav.

All rights reserved. No portion of this book may be reproduced—mechanically, electronically, or by any other means, including photocopying—without written permission
of the publisher.

Published by Blue Apron, Inc.
5 Crosby Street, 3rd Floor
New York, NY 10013
www.blueapron.com

Library of Congress Cataloguing-in-Publication Data
Spring Cooking with Blue Apron, A Collection of Simple, Seasonal Recipes: Vol. 1 / Blue Apron, Inc.—1st ed. p. cm.
ISBN 978-0-9905101-3-0

10 9 8 7 6 5 4 3 2 1

Printed in Canada by the Prolific Group

SPRING COOKING

WITH Blue Apron | A COLLECTION OF SIMPLE, SEASONAL RECIPES: *vol. 1*

Blue Apron

Contents

Welcome to the Blue Apron kitchen.

At Blue Apron, our mission is to make incredible home cooking accessible to everyone—to the novice cook just getting started and to the experienced chef who considers the kitchen home.

We create simple, seasonally-inspired recipes and send them to our customers every week, along with all the fresh ingredients—pre-measured and perfectly portioned—to prepare a delicious and healthy dinner.

In this cookbook, we celebrate our mission, while welcoming in the season, with our favorite spring ingredients and meals.

Why Eat at Home

We started Blue Apron to tackle cooking on a nightly basis, not just on special occasions. Even the simplest homemade salad or creative sandwich contains more whole, unprocessed ingredients than nearly anything pre-made. That translates into serious flavor and high-quality nutrition, as well as the measureless satisfaction of having created a wonderful meal. Cooking at home is a habit. Our goal is to make recipes that will inspire our customers to make it a part of their daily lives.

Step by Step

The weekly recipe cards we send with our ingredients contain up to six steps, accompanied by easy-to-follow photos. We've translated this visual cooking style into this book, so if you're not sure what to do after reading the text, take a close look at the corresponding photo for the visual cue. It will show you exactly how brown your caramelized onions should be or what we mean by "slightly reduced in volume."

Spring Ingredients

The earth is coming alive again. It's a unique season. The dormant seeds and trees begin to sprout and fruit. Berries are latticing the fields. Peas are climbing the trellises. Artichokes swell, preparing to blossom.

The burgeoning warmth along with its ample rains provide such a particular climate that certain plants are only available in spring: morel mushrooms, fiddlehead ferns and ramps.

In this book, we find pleasure not only in the ingredients, but what they stand for. The world is alive; the bounty of the land is beginning to ripen. And so much of it is already at its very best.

Lifelong Learning

The recipes in the first seven chapters of this book will help you master spring meals for two, but don't stop there! This volume also contains recipes for brand-new dishes and delicacies—including projects, desserts and feasts designed to serve ten or more. Each of these debut recipes has received the full Blue Apron treatment: inspired ingredients, accessible directions and step-by-step photos. As always, all you'll need to make them are the ingredients listed, along with olive oil, salt, pepper and a passion for great food!

How to Use This Cookbook

At Blue Apron, seasonality is one of our most treasured principles. That's why we've organized this cookbook around families of spring ingredients. From artichokes, to peas, to spring aromatics, to rhubarb and strawberries, to radishes, to ingredients that can only be found in the wild—each chapter explores the depth and versatility of the season's produce.

At the beginning of each chapter, we've included an essay that details the history of these groups, providing context and fun facts. We've also included a series of Field Guides that identify specific varieties and provide short descriptions. Also, throughout the volume, look for our Supplier Stories. These are profiles of some of the professionals we work with to source the best food available.

We're inspired by their stories, and we're inspired by yours! That's why we've included an entire spread of pictures you've shared with us—of you, your friends and your families preparing delicious, nutritious meals at home.

We can't wait to cook these spring recipes with you!

—THE BLUE APRON TEAM

WE WELCOME THE sight of spring. Our warm weather favorites are beginning to sprout. English peas and fava beans nestled in their pods; the spired bracts of artichokes curling towards their centers. Special produce like ramps and fiddlehead ferns, with their short seasons, remind us to treasure the moment and take advantage of this unique season before it passes.

Spring also provides us with the opportunity to celebrate life and renew our dedications. Let's begin the process again. Let's continue our growth through learning. Let's celebrate discovery, and rediscovery, both inside the kitchen and out.

We dedicate this book to you, our customers, who continually inspire and reinvigorate our mission.

—JUDITH PEÑA, CONTENT MANAGER

Asparagus

FIELD GUIDE TO ASPARAGUS

The following are some of our favorite heirloom and specialty varieties. The best place to find them is at your local farmers' market, or you can grow them. The seeds are available at seed saver websites.

Jersey Knight Asparagus: A tender variety developed on the East Coast. All asparagus bearing the name "Jersey" were developed by the Rutgers University agricultural program.

Mary Washington Asparagus: A cross of "Mary" and "Washington" strains. Produces the largest seeds and seedlings of any heirloom variety. One of the earliest varieties to shoot.

Precoce D'Argenteuil: An heirloom variety first grown in the 19th Century. The earliest sprouting of the D'Argenteuil varieties. First cultivated in Argenteuil, France, and prized for its tender and rosy, purple stalks.

Purple Passion Asparagus: A slender variety. Gets its pigmentation from high concentrations of anthocyanins (potent antioxidants found in many other purple vegetables).

White Asparagus: Made by covering regular green asparagus in a mound of soil after sprouting, depriving it of light and preventing photosynthesis from turning it green. Considered a delicacy throughout history.

Wild Asparagus: Characterized by its slender shoots. Like garlic, a member of the lily family. Native to much of Europe, North Africa and Western Asia.

ASPARAGUS IS A spring vegetable in the eponymously named *Asparagus* genus. It's actually the young shoot of a miniature evergreen tree, harvested before its flesh becomes woody. The spade-shaped "leaves" that line its long, narrow body are, in fact, early branches, preparing to reach out of a soon-to-be tree trunk.

In Turkish, the name for asparagus is "kuşkonmaz," which literally translates to "bird can't land." That's a decent description of the vegetable's shape, but what it leaves out is asparagus' exquisite tenderness. The delicate tips of the shoots are, in French, called "points d'amour," or "love tips." (For centuries, asparagus was thought to be an aphrodisiac, despite a lack of scientific evidence.)

In Ancient Rome, asparagus was considered a great delicacy. Mountaineers would climb high into the Alps to bury it in the snow, freezing it for summer festivals. But farming the plant has always been a challenge. After an asparagus field has been sown, the bed of soil sits for two years, unproductive. In the third year, edible shoots appear—but they only come up for a few seasons.

At any given time, growers have *half* their land empty, which has made asparagus relatively expensive.

In these recipes, we celebrate the plant's complex earthiness and lush, hearty texture, while displaying its beautiful color range, from green to violet-purple.

Shrimp Quinoa "Fried Rice"
with Asparagus & English Peas

This recipe, featuring asparagus and English peas, is a
sign that spring has officially arrived. Fried rice, the
traditional Chinese stir-fry dish, can be made with
countless different ingredients. But here, we're pushing
it to the limit—with delicious results. We're replacing
the rice itself with naturally nutty quinoa. Earthy,
complex asparagus makes the perfect pairing, and
English peas add incredible texture to this healthful
take on the classic.

MAKES 2 SERVINGS · ABOUT 690 CALORIES PER SERVING

Ingredients
3 Scallions
2 Cloves Garlic
1 1-Inch Piece Ginger
5-6 Sprigs Cilantro
1 Medium Carrot
½ Pound Asparagus
¼ Pound English Peas
1 Cup White Quinoa
10 Ounces Peeled & Deveined Shrimp, Tails Off
2 Tablespoons Mirin
2 Tablespoons Soy Sauce
2 Teaspoons Sesame Oil
2 Tablespoons Hoisin Sauce
1 Tablespoon Sambal Oelek

1 Prepare the ingredients

Wash and dry the fresh produce. Heat a medium pot of salted water to boiling on high. Cut off and discard the root ends of the scallions; thinly slice the scallions, separating the white bottoms and green tops. Peel and mince the garlic and ginger. Pick the cilantro leaves off the stems; discard the stems. Peel and small dice the carrot. Trim off and discard the woody bottoms of the asparagus; slice the asparagus into 1-inch pieces on angle. Shell the peas.

2 Cook the quinoa

Add the quinoa to the pot of boiling water. Cook 15 to 17 minutes, or until tender. Drain thoroughly and set aside.

3 Cook the shrimp

While the quinoa cooks, pat the shrimp dry with paper towels and season with salt and pepper. In a large pan (nonstick, if you have one), heat 2 teaspoons of oil on medium-high until hot. Add the seasoned shrimp and cook, stirring frequently, 2 to 3 minutes, or until opaque and cooked through. Transfer the cooked shrimp to a plate. Wipe out the pan.

4 Cook the vegetables

In the same pan used to cook the shrimp, heat 2 teaspoons of oil on medium until hot. Add the carrot and peas; season with salt and pepper. Cook, stirring occasionally, 2 to 3 minutes, or until the carrots have softened slightly. Add the garlic, ginger, white bottoms of the scallions and asparagus; season with salt and pepper. Cook, stirring frequently, 1 to 2 minutes, or until fragrant and the asparagus is slightly softened.

5 Finish & plate your dish

To the pan of vegetables, add the cooked quinoa, cooked shrimp and half the green tops of the scallions; stir to combine. Add the mirin, soy sauce, sesame oil, half the hoisin sauce and as much of the sambal oelek as you'd like, depending on how spicy you'd like the dish to be. Cook, stirring occasionally, 2 to 4 minutes, or until the liquid has been absorbed. (If the mixture starts to stick to the bottom of the pan, use a spatula to scrape it up.) Remove from heat. To plate your dish, divide the "fried rice" between 2 dishes. Garnish with the cilantro, remaining green tops of the scallions and remaining hoisin sauce.

Asparagus & Spring Onion Tart
with Arugula & Mâche Salad

This savory, light tart is the perfect celebration of spring. We used the first ripe harvest of asparagus, pairing it with spring onions (onions picked early, beloved for their delicate flavor). You'll make a quick and easy, rich and flaky crust using whole wheat flour and olive oil. A filling of vegetables, farm fresh eggs and sweet, slightly salty Gruyere even out this wonderful, festive meal with arugula and mâche (a bunched, sweet-tasting, leafy green).

MAKES 2 SERVINGS · ABOUT 700 CALORIES PER SERVING

Ingredients

2 Cloves Garlic
2 Ounces Gruyere Cheese
2 Spring Onions
½ Pound Asparagus
3-4 Sprigs Parsley
1 Lemon
½ Cup All-Purpose Flour
½ Cup Whole Wheat Flour
2 Eggs
1 Tablespoon Whole Grain Dijon Mustard
½ Cup Low-Fat Milk
2 Ounces Arugula
1 Ounce Mâche

1 Prepare the ingredients

Preheat the oven to 375°F. Wash and dry the fresh produce. Peel and thinly slice the garlic. Grate the Gruyere cheese. Separate the white bulbs and green tops of the spring onions; cut the bulbs into ½-inch wedges and thinly slice the green parts on an angle. Trim off and discard the woody bottoms of the asparagus; cut the asparagus into 2-inch pieces on an angle. Pick the parsley leaves off the stems; discard the stems. Using a peeler, remove the yellow rind of the lemon, avoiding the white pith; mince the rind to get 2 teaspoons of zest. Quarter the lemon and remove the seeds.

2 Make & pre-bake the crust

In a medium bowl, combine the all-purpose and whole wheat flours. Stir in ¼ cup of olive oil and ¼ cup of cold water just until the dough forms a soft ball, being careful not to over-mix. Cover the bottom and sides of an oven-safe baking dish by gently pressing the dough into it; using a fork, poke a few holes in the dough. Bake 13 to 15 minutes, or until lightly browned. Remove from the oven and set aside. Increase the oven temperature to 425°F.

3 Cook the vegetables

While the crust bakes, in a large pan, heat 2 teaspoons of olive oil on medium until hot. Add the garlic, white parts of the spring onions and asparagus; season with salt and pepper. Cook, stirring occasionally, 3 to 4 minutes, or until the asparagus is tender and bright green and the onions are slightly softened. Transfer to a plate.

4 Assemble & bake the tart

In a medium bowl, whisk together the eggs, lemon zest, mustard, milk, half the parsley (roughly chopping before adding) and all but a pinch of the Gruyere cheese. Continue whisking until well combined; season with salt and pepper. Once slightly cooled, stir in the cooked spring onion and asparagus. Pour the filling into the pre-baked crust. Sprinkle the remaining cheese on top of the filling. Bake 20 to 22 minutes, or until the filling is completely set and the top is browned. (Depending on the depth of your baking dish, cooking times may vary; monitor carefully.) Remove from the oven and let stand for at least 5 minutes before serving.

5 Dress the greens & plate your dish

In a large bowl, toss the arugula, mâche and half the green parts of the onions with a drizzle of olive oil and the juice of 2 lemon wedges (you will have extra lemon wedges); season with salt and pepper to taste. To plate your dish, divide the tart between 2 plates. Serve with the dressed salad on the side. Garnish the tart with the remaining parsley and green parts of the onion.

The Asparagus Delta: Zuckerman's Farm

AN HOUR AND a half east of San Francisco, where the San Joaquin and Sacramento rivers flow together, Roscoe Zuckerman bends down to examine an asparagus spear in a field plowed with rich, dark furrows.

"Few people really know how asparagus is grown," says Roscoe, severing the base of the stalk with a special forked knife designed for this purpose. He lifts the bract-lined vegetable up to examine its girth: the wider the asparagus, the longer it has been in the ground, and the more flavor it promises.

Asparagus is one of the most difficult crops to grow—at least, when it's grown with care, as it is at Zuckerman's Farm. The plant can take years to reach maturity, meaning that fields will spend a significant amount of time lying fallow. Harvesting the spears too early, before they're plump, means sacrificing the essence of the crop. And that's something Roscoe shakes his head at.

"Here at Zuckerman's," he says, "we insist on growing asparagus the right way. The way it's been grown for countless generations."

And generations are something Roscoe and his siblings know a thing or two about. The farm is nearly 100 years old, and just about every member of the family has been involved in helping out since its inception.

Surrounded by bays and levees, Zuckerman's is situated in a unique landscape, and it's run by a uniquely talented group of people.

"I love this field," says Roscoe, looking out across the acres of stalks.

We couldn't agree more, for Zuckerman's asparagus is some of the best we've ever tasted.

Pork Milanese

with Bacon, Escarole, Cannellini Beans & Asparagus

In this springtime spin on an Italian classic, we're letting asparagus' incredible flavor speak for itself. As a topping for the rest of the dish, we're dressing thinly sliced, raw asparagus with fresh lemon juice and tarragon. We're also serving up a uniquely flavorful sauté that combines crispy bacon, white beans and crunchy escarole. There's no better way to cut the richness of pork Milanese (lightly fried, breaded cutlets).

MAKES 2 SERVINGS • ABOUT 700 CALORIES PER SERVING

Ingredients
2 5-Ounce Pork Cutlets
2 Slices Bacon
6 Ounces Escarole (About 1 Head)
5 Ounces Asparagus
1 Lemon
1 Red Onion
3-4 Sprigs Tarragon
3 Tablespoons Smooth Dijon Mustard
1 Cup Canned White Cannellini Beans
¾ Cup Panko Breadcrumbs

1 Prepare the ingredients

Wash and dry the fresh produce. Remove the pork from the refrigerator to bring to room temperature. Small dice the bacon. Remove and discard the root end of the escarole; roughly chop the leaves. Cut off and discard the woody bottoms of the asparagus; very thinly slice the stalks on an angle. Using a peeler, remove the yellow rind of the lemon, avoiding the white pith; mince the rind to get 2 teaspoons of zest. Quarter the lemon and remove the seeds. Peel and thinly slice the onion. Pick the tarragon leaves off the stems; discard the stems and finely chop the leaves. In a shallow dish, stir together the mustard and ¼ cup of water.

2 Cook the bacon

In a large pan, heat 1 teaspoon of olive oil on medium until hot. Add the bacon and cook, stirring occasionally, 3 to 5 minutes, or until browned.

3 Add the vegetables

To the pan of bacon, add the escarole, lemon zest and onion; season with salt and pepper. Cook, stirring occasionally, 2 to 3 minutes, or until the escarole is slightly wilted. Add the beans and ¼ cup of water; cook, stirring occasionally, 1 to 2 minutes, or until heated through. Remove from heat and stir in the juice of 1 lemon wedge; season with salt and pepper to taste.

4 Cook the pork

Place the breadcrumbs on a plate. Season the pork with salt and pepper on both sides. Working one at a time, thoroughly coat both sides of each seasoned pork cutlet in the mustard-water mixture (letting the excess drip off), then the breadcrumbs (letting the excess fall off). Transfer to a plate. Repeat with the remaining pork cutlet. In a medium pan (nonstick, if you have one), heat a thin layer of oil on medium-high until hot. When the oil is hot enough that a few breadcrumbs sizzle immediately when added to the pan, add the coated pork cutlets. Cook 2 to 3 minutes per side, or until browned and cooked through. Transfer to a paper towel-lined plate.

5 Finish & plate your dish

In a medium bowl, combine the asparagus, tarragon and the juice of 1 lemon wedge. Add a drizzle of olive oil and toss to coat; season with salt and pepper to taste. To plate your dish, divide the pork and cooked bacon and vegetables between 2 plates. Top with the dressed asparagus. Garnish with the remaining lemon wedges.

Soft-Boiled Eggs over Risotto-Style Red Quinoa
with Sautéed Asparagus

This dish is our seasonal take on a French classic: soft-boiled eggs with asparagus. The velvety yolks of soft-boiled eggs go perfectly with the tender snap and fresh, subtle taste of asparagus. In our version, you'll serve the eggs on a bed of lemony red quinoa (cooked risotto-style) to soak up the golden yolk. With a zesty baby kale salad to top it off, this meal is elegantly delicious.

MAKES 2 SERVINGS • ABOUT 700 CALORIES PER SERVING

Ingredients

2 Eggs
1 2-Ounce Block Parmesan Cheese
1 Pound Asparagus
1 Lemon
2 Cloves Garlic
1 Shallot
1 Cup Red Quinoa
3 Tablespoons Vegetable Demi-Glace
1 Tablespoon Smooth Dijon Mustard
2 Ounces Baby Kale

1 Prepare the ingredients
Wash and dry the fresh produce. Remove the eggs from the refrigerator to bring to room temperature. Heat a medium pot of water to boiling on high. Grate half the Parmesan cheese; leave the rest in a block. Cut off and discard the woody bottoms of the asparagus stems. Using a peeler, remove the yellow rind of the lemon, avoiding the white pith; mince the rind to get 2 teaspoons of zest. Quarter the lemon and remove the seeds. Peel and mince the garlic and shallot. Place half the shallot in a small bowl with the juice of all 4 lemon wedges. Thoroughly rinse the quinoa under cold water; drain thoroughly.

2 Cook the asparagus
In a medium pan, heat 2 teaspoons of olive oil on medium-high until hot. Add the asparagus and season with salt and pepper. Cook, stirring occasionally, 2 to 3 minutes, or until bright green and slightly tender. Transfer to a plate and set aside. Wipe out the pan.

3 Cook the quinoa & make the vinaigrette
In the same pan used to cook the asparagus, heat 2 teaspoons of olive oil on medium until hot. Add the garlic and remaining shallot and cook, stirring frequently, 30 seconds to 1 minute, or until softened and fragrant. Add the quinoa and toast, stirring frequently, 30 seconds to 1 minute, or until nuttily fragrant. Add the vegetable demi-glace, lemon zest and 3 cups of water; season with salt and pepper. Cook, stirring occasionally, 20 to 22 minutes, or until the quinoa is tender and cooked through. Remove from heat. Off the heat, stir in the grated Parmesan cheese. While the quinoa cooks, add the mustard to the shallot-lemon juice mixture and season with salt and pepper. Whisk in 2 tablespoons of olive oil until well combined. Set aside.

4 Cook the eggs
While the quinoa continues to cook, add the eggs to the pot of boiling water and cook for exactly 5 minutes. Drain and rinse under cold water for 30 seconds to 1 minute to stop the cooking process. When cool enough to handle, carefully peel the eggs and set aside.

5 Finish & plate your dish
In a medium bowl, toss the kale with enough of the vinaigrette to coat the greens (you may have extra vinaigrette); season with salt and pepper to taste. To plate your dish, divide the finished quinoa between 2 plates and top each with the cooked asparagus, dressed kale and soft-boiled eggs. Using a peeler, shave the remaining Parmesan cheese over the salad.

Wild

FIELD GUIDE TO WILD PRODUCE

The following are some of our favorite heirloom and specialty varieties. The best place to buy them is at your local farmers' market.

Dandelion: The common, herbaceous perennial plant sometimes regarded as a weed. Edible in its entirety and prized for the unique flavor of its leaves and flowers. Native to most of North America, South America and Eurasia.

Fiddleheads: The furled fronds of a fern. Harvested when young, before the leaves have a chance to develop. Only available seasonally.

Miner's Lettuce: Can be found along the western mountain and coastal regions of the United States, but most prevalent in the valleys of California. Not actually a form of lettuce. Eaten by Gold Rush miners because of its high concentration of Vitamin C to ward off scurvy.

Morels: A delightful mushroom with a honeycomb-like cap. In the United States, fruits along with the warmer weather spring brings. Almost impossible to cultivate. Most are foraged in the wild.

Nasturtium: A flower native to South America. All parts of it are edible. Produces an essential oil similar to that produced by watercress. Often used as a salad green or an ornamental garnish.

Ramps: Found growing wild across most of the Eastern United States. A kind of wild onion in the same family as leeks and garlic. In some folklore, ramps are the true sign that spring has arrived. Considered a gourmet vegetable.

Stinging Nettles: Found worldwide. Soaking or cooking nettles will remove the stinging chemicals. The plant can then be used as a leafy green. Among greens, extremely high in protein.

Wood Sorrel: Named for its resemblance to the common sorrel herb, though the two are unrelated. An edible plant eaten around the world for millennia. Popular in Native American cuisines, and occasionally used for its medicinal properties.

AS IT WAKES from the drowsiness of winter, nature is bustling with new life. Conditions are perfect. In fact, there are some plants and mushrooms that require such specific environments that they're *only* available during a short window in spring. Ramps, morel mushrooms, fiddlehead ferns and purslane are among them.

Ramps (also known as wild leeks) are only available in the wild and are only ripe in spring. Native peoples in the area of what is now Chicago called the ramp "chicagou" and actually named the river for the copious amounts of ramps that grew along it. The name of the present-day city echoes this past profusion.

The morel, characterized by its honeycomb-patterned cap, is another spring specialty. Spring

rains in forests and fields provide the perfect conditions for it to sprout. It is nearly impossible to cultivate the morel. Its scarcity—and delicious, earthy flavor—has made it a prized commodity throughout North America and Europe.

Fiddleheads are the furled fronds of a very specific kind of fern. They can only be harvested in spring when they're young, before the leaves unroll. Because of this short harvesting period, fiddleheads aren't cultivated, though they grow almost the world over.

Purslane is incredibly widespread on the North American continent. (Some of you might even have it growing in your backyard right now!) Spring is the best time to take advantage of its unique, herbaceous, lemony and slightly briny flavor.

Chicken Supremes
with Ramps, Snap Peas & Mashed Sweet Potatoes

This thoroughly springy dish uses ramps, also known as wild leeks. They're a delicately-flavored vegetable with a strong garlicky aroma and a mild, onion-like flavor. In certain parts of the Eastern U.S. and Appalachia, spring is celebrated with the arrival of the ramp, and some believe it to be a wonder tonic that bolsters health and wards off all kinds of ailments.

MAKES 2 SERVINGS • ABOUT 535 CALORIES PER SERVING

Ingredients

2 8-Ounce Chicken Supremes (Bone-In, Skin-On Breasts)
6 Ounces Sugar Snap Peas
2 Cloves Garlic
2 Ounces Ramps
1 Lemon
1 Pound Sweet Potatoes
2 Tablespoons Butter
3 Sprigs Lemon Thyme

1 Prepare the ingredients

Wash and dry the fresh produce. Heat a large pot of salted water to boiling on high. Remove the chicken from the refrigerator to bring to room temperature. Trim off and discard the ends of the snap peas; slice each pea in half on an angle. Peel and thinly slice the garlic. Trim off and discard the roots of the ramps; if any dirt is noticeable, wash the ramps again until clean. Roughly chop the white bottoms and green leaves of the ramps. Quarter the lemon and remove the seeds. Peel and large dice the sweet potatoes.

2 Cook the sweet potatoes

Once the pot of water is boiling, add the sweet potatoes. Cook 14 to 16 minutes, or until very tender when pierced with a fork. Drain thoroughly and return to the pot. Add half the butter and a drizzle of olive oil. Using a fork, mash the cooked sweet potatoes until smooth; season with salt and pepper to taste. Set aside in a warm place.

3 Start the chicken

While the sweet potatoes cook, pat the chicken dry with paper towels and season both sides with salt and pepper. In a large pan, heat 2 teaspoons of olive oil on medium-high until hot. Add the seasoned chicken, skin side down first; loosely cover the pan with aluminum foil. Cook 4 to 6 minutes on the first side, or until browned.

4 Finish the chicken

Flip the chicken and cook 4 to 6 minutes, or until browned and cooked through. Remove the pan from heat. Off the heat, add the garlic, lemon thyme sprigs and remaining butter. Once the butter has melted, spoon the sauce over the chicken until thoroughly coated. Transfer the cooked chicken to a plate. Remove and discard the lemon thyme sprigs, leaving the garlic and any chicken drippings in the pan.

5 Cook the vegetables & plate your dish

Add 2 teaspoons of olive oil to the pan of garlic and chicken drippings and heat on medium until hot. Add the ramps and cook, stirring frequently, 30 seconds to 1 minute, or until fragrant and slightly softened. Add the snap peas; cook, stirring occasionally, 2 to 3 minutes, or until bright green and slightly tender. Season with salt and pepper to taste. To plate your dish, slice the chicken breasts crosswise on an angle. Divide the mashed sweet potatoes and sautéed vegetables between 2 plates. Top each with the juice of 1 lemon wedge and a drizzle of olive oil. Garnish with the remaining lemon wedges.

Steamed Cod
with Pickled Ramps & Yu Choy

In this recipe, we're putting a spin on spring. Ramps, long considered one of the first signs of spring, are incredibly flavorful. In this recipe, we're pickling them in a brine with coconut palm sugar and rice vinegar to mellow their oniony flavor and provide a bright, tart kick. To round out the flavor profile, yu choy, a leafy vegetable in the mustard family, adds the perfect peppery bite to the flavors of this dish.

MAKES 2 SERVINGS • ABOUT 500 CALORIES PER SERVING

Ingredients
2 5-Ounce Cod Fillets
2 Cloves Garlic
2 Ounces Ramps
½ Pound Yu Choy
5-6 Sprigs Cilantro
1 1-Inch Piece Ginger
1 Cup Brown Rice
¼ Cup Rice Wine Vinegar, Unseasoned
2 Tablespoons Coconut Palm Sugar
1 Tablespoon Soy Sauce

1 Prepare the ingredients

Wash and dry the fresh produce. Remove the cod from the refrigerator to bring to room temperature. Peel and thinly slice the garlic. Trim off and discard the roots of the ramps. If any dirt is noticeable, wash the ramps again until clean. Separate the white bottoms and green tops of the ramps; roughly chop the green tops. Trim off and discard the ends of the yu choy; roughly chop the leaves. Pick the cilantro leaves off the stems; discard the stems. Peel and cut the ginger into thin matchsticks.

2 Cook the rice

In a small pot, combine the rice, a big pinch of salt and 2 cups of water. Heat to boiling on high. Once boiling, cover and reduce the heat to low. Cook 18 to 20 minutes, or until the water is absorbed and the rice is tender. Remove from heat. Fluff the finished rice with a fork.

3 Pickle the ramps

While the rice cooks, place the white bottoms of the ramps in a heatproof bowl or container. In a medium pan (nonstick, if you have one), combine half of the rice wine vinegar, half of the coconut palm sugar and 2 tablespoons of water. Cook on medium heat, occasionally swirling the pan, 1 to 2 minutes, or until the sugar has dissolved. Pour the pickling liquid over the white bottoms of the ramps. Set aside. Wipe out the pan.

4 Cook the vegetables & steam the fish

In the same pan used to make the pickling liquid, heat 2 teaspoons of oil on medium-high until hot. Add the garlic. Cook, stirring occasionally, 1 to 2 minutes, or until golden brown and fragrant. Add the yu choy and green tops of the ramps; season with salt and pepper. Cook, stirring frequently, 2 to 3 minutes, or until wilted. While the vegetables cook, pat the cod fillets dry and season with salt and pepper on both sides. Add the seasoned cod and ½ cup of water to the pan of vegetables. Cook, loosely covering with aluminum foil, 6 to 7 minutes, or until the cod is opaque and cooked through. Divide the fish and vegetables between 2 dishes. Set aside in a warm place. Wipe out the pan.

5 Make the ginger-soy sauce & plate your dish

In the same pan used to steam the fish, heat 2 teaspoons of oil on medium-high until hot. Add the ginger and cook, stirring occasionally, 1 to 2 minutes, or until softened and fragrant. Add the soy sauce, remaining rice wine vinegar and remaining palm sugar. Cook, stirring constantly, 30 seconds to 1 minute, or until thoroughly combined. Remove from heat. Divide the cooked rice between the dishes of fish and vegetables. Spoon the ginger-soy sauce over the top. Garnish with the pickled ramps and cilantro.

Ramping It Up: Lucky Dog Farms

THE MURMUR OF the Delaware River cuts a valley through the Catskill mountains. The rocky hills that surround it are lush with green as the river swells. The soil, a deep loam deposited by glaciers and the river itself, creates a special environment for growers.

Among this incredibly fertile landscape, Lucky Dog Farm owner Richard Giles surveys his land, and his crops, some of which, even this early in spring, are beginning to ripen.

Originally from the South, where he managed farms, Rich was taken by the picturesque landscape on a visit to northern New York. In fact, he was so taken that he moved there, buying his first plot of land in the spring of 2000.

"Ramps have always been a sign of something," he says, "especially in the Appalachians." At Lucky Dog, spring heaps incredible amounts of ramps upon the Earth. Richard and his wife, along with their small team of local farmers, live with the land, cultivating and caring for the plants using sustainable techniques. They make their own compost and only plant truly organic vegetables.

"Our goal is to provide high-quality, nutritious, organic produce for our immediate community and downstate neighbors," Rich says. Quality has always been the bottom line at Lucky Dog. Rich's experience, coupled with the unique land, yield incredible results. Their ramps are, for lack of a better term, perfect.

Flank Steak

with Ramps, Fingerling Potatoes & Shaved Asparagus Salad

Let's welcome in spring with a feast of seasonal vegetables! From ramps to fingerlings to asparagus, this dish has it all. Ramps, the garlicky onion relative, are perfect for flavoring delicate fingerlings (small, tasty potatoes) and earthy, complex asparagus. We're using the asparagus two ways. First, we're shaving off the sides of the spears to make thin ribbons for a tender salad. But we're also reserving the shaved spears for a delicious vegetable sauté that makes the perfect side for juicy flank steaks served with lemon crème fraîche.

MAKES 2 SERVINGS • ABOUT 640 CALORIES PER SERVING

Ingredients

2 5-Ounce Flank Steaks
7 Ounces Asparagus
4 Ounces Ramps
1 Lemon
½ Pound Fingerling Potatoes
2 Sprigs Dill
1 Small Bunch Chives
1 Shallot
4 Tablespoons Butter
¼ Cup Crème Fraîche

1 Prepare the ingredients

Wash and dry the fresh produce. Remove the steaks from the refrigerator to bring to room temperature. Using a peeler, shave off some of the asparagus to get thin ribbons; reserve the spears and place the shaved asparagus in a bowl. Trim off and discard the roots of the ramps. If any dirt becomes noticeable, rinse the ramps again. Roughly chop the white bottoms and green leaves of the ramps. Using a peeler, remove the yellow rind of the lemon, avoiding the white pith; mince the rind to get 2 teaspoons of zest. Quarter the lemon and remove the seeds. Halve the potatoes lengthwise. Pick the dill off the stems; discard the stems. Roughly chop the chives. Peel and thinly slice the shallot. In a small bowl, combine the sliced shallot and the juice of all 4 lemon wedges. In a separate small bowl, combine the crème fraîche and half the lemon zest; season with salt and pepper to taste.

2 Cook the potatoes

In a large pan, heat 2 teaspoons of olive oil on medium-high until hot. Add the potatoes and season with salt and pepper. Cook, flipping occasionally, 7 to 9 minutes, or until golden brown and tender when pierced with a fork. Transfer to a plate and set aside. Wipe out the pan.

3 Cook the steaks

Pat the steaks dry with paper towels. Season the steaks with salt and pepper on both sides. In the same pan used to cook the potatoes, heat 2 teaspoons of olive oil on medium until hot. Add the seasoned steaks. Cook 3 to 4 minutes on the first side. Flip the steaks and add the butter. Cook, occasionally tilting the pan and spooning the melted butter over the steaks, 2 to 4 minutes, or until the steaks are cooked to your desired degree of doneness. Transfer to a cutting board and let rest for at least 5 minutes. Wipe out the pan.

4 Cook the vegetables

In the same pan used to cook the steaks, heat 2 teaspoons of olive oil on medium-high until hot. Add the asparagus spears, ramps, remaining lemon zest and cooked potatoes; season with salt and pepper. Cook, stirring occasionally, 4 to 6 minutes, or until the ramps are slightly wilted and the asparagus is bright green. Remove from heat and set aside in a warm place.

5 Make the salad & plate your dish

In a large bowl, combine the shaved asparagus, marinated shallot and dill; season with salt and pepper. Drizzle with olive oil and toss to thoroughly coat. Divide the cooked vegetables between 2 plates. Top with the steaks and shaved asparagus salad. Garnish with the chives. Serve with the lemon crème fraîche on the side.

Braised Wild Mushrooms over Barley
with Morels, Toasted Breadcrumbs & Parmesan Cheese

Spring is the season of mushrooms. For this tasty dish, we're pairing morel mushrooms (one of our favorite specialty types) with mixed, wild varieties. One of these is the delicate maitake, also known as "hen-of-the-woods." This gorgeous delicacy is easily identified by its overlapping caps, which are arranged like the feathers of a bird. The name maitake is Japanese and translates to "dancing mushroom." In the wild, it is said to resemble the waving hands and rippling kimono sleeves of dancers. Whatever they remind you of, these mushrooms are delicious!

MAKES 2 SERVINGS • ABOUT 580 CALORIES PER SERVING

Ingredients

2 Fresh Morel Mushrooms
8 Ounces Mixed Wild Mushrooms
    (Maitake & Oyster)
4 Cloves Garlic
3-4 Sprigs Parsley
2 Sprigs Thyme
1 Carrot
1 Yellow Onion
1 Cup Pearled Barley
¼ Cup Panko Breadcrumbs
1 Cup Vegetable Broth
4 Tablespoons Butter
1 Tablespoon Sherry Vinegar
½ Cup Grated Parmesan Cheese

1 Prepare the ingredients

Wash and dry the fresh produce. Heat a medium pot of salted water to boiling on high. Cut the morel, maitake and oyster mushrooms into large pieces. Peel and mince the garlic. Pick the parsley and thyme leaves off the stems; discard the stems. Peel and small dice the carrot and onion.

2 Cook the barley

Add the barley to the pot of boiling water. Cook 20 to 22 minutes, or until tender. Drain thoroughly and return to the pot. Drizzle with olive oil and stir to thoroughly combine; season with salt and pepper to taste.

3 Toast the breadcrumbs

While the barley cooks, heat a large, dry pan on medium-high until hot. Add the breadcrumbs and toast, stirring frequently, 2 to 3 minutes, or until lightly browned. Transfer to a bowl and set aside. Wipe out the pan.

4 Cook the mushrooms

In the same pan used to toast the breadcrumbs, heat 2 teaspoons of olive oil on medium-high until hot. Add the morel, maitake and oyster mushrooms in a single, even layer. Cook 3 to 4 minutes, or until slightly crispy; season with salt and pepper. Transfer to a paper towel-lined plate and set aside. Wipe out the pan.

5 Finish & plate your dish

In the same pan used to cook the mushrooms, heat 2 teaspoons of olive oil on medium-high until hot. Add the onion and garlic and cook, stirring frequently, 2 to 3 minutes, or until fragrant and softened. Add the carrot and season with salt and pepper. Cook, stirring occasionally, 2 to 3 minutes, or until softened. Reduce the heat to medium and add the cooked mushrooms, vegetable broth and thyme; season with salt and pepper. Cook, stirring occasionally, 2 to 4 minutes, or until the liquid has reduced slightly. Remove from heat. Off the heat, stir in the butter, sherry vinegar and half the Parmesan cheese; season with salt and pepper to taste. To plate your dish, divide the cooked barley between 2 dishes and top with the mushroom stew. Garnish with the parsley, toasted breadcrumbs and remaining Parmesan cheese.

Mushroom, Leek & Potato Gratin
with Morels & Arugula-Radish Salad

Morel mushrooms, prized by many of the world's best chefs for their earthy complexity, can turn even the simplest recipe into a gourmet meal brimming with flavor. In this delicious dish, we rehydrated dried morels in water, then used the water as the base of a creamy, tasty béchamel sauce. For the filling of the gratin, we used the morel mushrooms themselves. And we're serving the gratin with a springtime salad featuring peppery radishes dressed with a simple, classic vinaigrette.

MAKES 2 SERVINGS • ABOUT 625 CALORIES PER SERVING

Ingredients

1 Pound Yukon Gold Potatoes
6 Ounces King Trumpet Mushrooms
3 Ounces Radishes, Without Greens
1 Leek
2 Sprigs Thyme
3 Ounces Piave Cheese
¼ Ounce Dried Morel Mushrooms
2 Tablespoons All-Purpose Flour
1 Cup Low-Fat Milk
1 Tablespoon Red Wine Vinegar
2 Ounces Arugula

1 Prepare the ingredients

Preheat the oven to 450°F. Wash and dry the fresh produce. Heat a medium pot of salted water to boiling on high. Peel and medium dice the potatoes. Small dice the king trumpet mushrooms. Halve and thinly slice the radishes. Trim off and discard the roots and upper, dark-green leaves of the leek; halve the leek lengthwise and rinse thoroughly. Small dice the leek. Pick the thyme leaves off the stems; discard the stems and roughly chop the leaves. Remove and discard the rind of the Piave cheese; grate the cheese. In a small bowl, combine the morel mushrooms and 1 cup of hot water. Let stand for at least 10 minutes.

2 Cook the potatoes & vegetables

Add the potatoes to the pot of boiling water. Cook 8 to 10 minutes, or until tender when pierced with a fork. Drain thoroughly and set aside. While the potatoes cook, in a separate, medium pot, heat 2 teaspoons of olive oil on medium-high until hot. Add the king trumpet mushrooms and leek; season with salt and pepper. Cook, stirring occasionally, 5 to 7 minutes, or until the mushrooms are slightly browned and the leek has softened.

3 Make the filling

Add 1 tablespoon of olive oil and the flour to the pot of vegetables; reduce the heat to medium. Cook, stirring frequently, 1 to 2 minutes, or until the flour is toasted and fragrant. Remove the morel mushrooms from the bowl of hot water; set the morels aside and reserve the water. Add the milk and morel water to the pan of vegetables and flour. Cook, stirring occasionally, 3 to 5 minutes, or until slightly thickened. Add the cooked potatoes, morel mushrooms (roughly chopping just before adding), half the Piave cheese and all but a pinch of the thyme; season with salt and pepper. Cook, stirring occasionally, 2 to 4 minutes, or until well combined and heated through. Remove from heat.

4 Assemble & bake the gratin

Transfer the filling to an oven-safe baking dish. Evenly distribute the remaining Piave cheese over top. Bake 12 to 14 minutes, or until lightly browned. Let stand for 2 minutes before serving.

5 Make the salad & plate your dish

Place the vinegar in a small bowl and season with salt and pepper to taste. Slowly whisk in 2 tablespoons of olive oil until well combined. In a medium bowl, combine the arugula and radishes. Add enough of the vinaigrette to coat the greens (you may have extra vinaigrette); toss to mix. Garnish the gratin with the remaining thyme. Serve with the salad on the side.

Whole Wheat Spaghetti
with Fiddleheads, Cannellini Beans & Purple Spring Onions

Fiddleheads are the curled fronds of young ferns, harvested in spring before the leaves have a chance to grow and unroll. The name "fiddlehead" comes from their resemblance to the scroll (the spiraled, decorative top) of a violin or fiddle. Along with purple spring onions, this incredible ingredient provides a simple, elegant touch to this wholesome pasta.

MAKES 2 SERVINGS • ABOUT 700 CALORIES PER SERVING

Ingredients

3 Cloves Garlic
6 Ounces Purple Spring Onions (About 2)
1 15-Ounce Can Cannellini Beans
2 Sprigs Lemon Basil
1 Lemon
2 Ounces Fiddlehead Ferns
8 Ounces Dried Whole Wheat Spaghetti
2 Tablespoons Butter
¼ Cup Grated Parmesan Cheese

1 Prepare the ingredients
Wash and dry the fresh produce. Heat a large pot of salted water to boiling on high. Peel and mince the garlic. Cut off the roots and green tips of the spring onions; discard the roots and all but a pinch of the green tips. Peel off and discard the spring onions' outermost layers; thinly slice the onions on an angle. Drain and rinse the beans. Pick the basil leaves off the stems; discard the stems. Using a peeler, remove the yellow rind of the lemon, avoiding the white pith; mince the rind to get 2 teaspoons of zest. Quarter the lemon and remove the seeds.

2 Prepare the fiddleheads
Cut off and discard the woody ends of the fiddleheads. Working one at a time, unroll each fern; remove and discard any dirt or fuzzy parts. Submerge the fiddleheads in cold water and swish them around to remove any fuzz still clinging to them; thoroughly drain. Repeat until the fiddleheads come out completely clean. Transfer to a paper towel and set aside.

3 Cook the pasta
Once the pot of water is boiling, add the pasta. Cook 9 to 11 minutes, or until just shy of al dente (still slightly firm to the bite). Reserve 1 cup of the pasta cooking water; drain the pasta thoroughly. Set aside.

4 Cook the fiddleheads
In a large pan (nonstick, if you have one), heat 2 teaspoons of olive oil on medium-high until hot. Add the fiddleheads and cook 2 to 3 minutes, or until browned.

5 Finish & plate your dish
Add the garlic and white bottoms of the spring onions to the pan of fiddleheads. Cook, stirring frequently, 30 seconds to 1 minute, or until softened and fragrant. Add the cooked pasta, beans, lemon zest, the juice of 2 lemon wedges and ½ cup of the reserved pasta water. Cook, tossing to coat, 1 to 2 minutes, or until the liquid has been absorbed. (If the sauce seems dry, slowly add the remaining pasta water until you achieve your desired consistency.) Remove from heat. Off the heat, stir in the butter, lemon basil (roughly chopping the leaves just before adding) and half the Parmesan cheese; stir to thoroughly combine and season with salt and pepper to taste. To plate your dish, divide the finished pasta between 2 plates. Garnish with the green tips of the onions and remaining Parmesan cheese and lemon wedges.

Peas
& Fava Beans

FIELD GUIDE TO PEAS & FAVA BEANS

The following are some of our favorite heirloom and specialty varieties. The best place to find them is at your local farmers' market, or you can grow them. The seeds are available at seed saver websites.

Aquadulce Fava Bean: An heirloom Spanish variety that produces large, white, sweet beans. Literally translates from Italian as "sweet water." So named because of its delicate flavor and pale hue.

Green Arrow Pea: English heirloom variety. Thrives in cool weather and is ready and mature in early spring. Derived from the common peas that were a staple of Medieval cuisines.

Pea Shoots: The sprouts of the English pea plant. Can be used as a salad green. Remarkably fresh-tasting and versatile.

Pea Tendrils: The young, spindly shoots of the pea plant. These vines would eventually grow into beanstalks and bean pods.

Shiraz Purple Snow Pea: A relatively new addition to the market. Developed in the early 2000s. Contains an abundance of antioxidants.

Snow Pea: Native to the Mediterranean. From there spread to China where it became the pea of choice. Still essential to the cuisines of certain regions in China.

Sugar Snap Pea: Sweetest, highest yielding pea. Many of the varieties we see today were developed in the 1960s in an attempt to create a pea that didn't need to be shelled.

PEAS ARE THE taste of spring. And there are so many ways to use them. Technically a kind of legume (like beans or lentils), the little green globes we most readily associate with the term are native to Western Asia. They've been cultivated since the Bronze Age and spread to India and China by the 7th Century. (In Chinese, the word for pea translates to "foreign legume.") During that time, peas, also called "field peas," were quickly becoming a staple of European cuisine, which featured almost exclusively the pea itself (the seed of the plant).

But there are so many other ways to eat peas! In the 16th Century, field peas were selectively and successfully cultivated for tenderness—meaning that the pod could be eaten as well. These tender "garden" peas (also called "sugar" or "snap" peas)

took Europe by storm. In 17th-Century Paris, they were considered exceptionally fashionable.

Since then, we've rediscovered other parts of the pea plant as well. Pea shoots, the edible leaves, are full of flavor. Pea tendrils, the wispy sprouts, are a delicate, elegant addition to meals. This chapter celebrates all forms of the pea, bringing back a little of the rage.

Here, we're also including another of our favorite "shelled" vegetables: fava beans. They're one of the oldest cultivated vegetables and one of the easiest to grow. Recipes for fava bean soups date back to the 1st Century. Some believe that these beans saved the population of Sicily from starvation in the Middle Ages. In spring, they're at their absolute best.

Chicken & Snow Pea-Radish Sauté
with Candied Pistachios

Snow peas are incredible sautéed. The hot pan caramelizes them slightly, bringing out their natural sweetness. And in this recipe, that's perfect, because we're giving you a primer in candy-making. To make a crunchy, sweet topping, you'll candy pistachios with caramel. But you'll be doing it the easy way: dissolving the sugar in water and boiling it down to a perfect amber color. It's a classic technique and the basis of literally every caramel-based confection. (Be sure to keep a watchful eye. Sugar can go from perfect amber to overcooked fairly quickly.)

MAKES 2 SERVINGS • ABOUT 555 CALORIES PER SERVING

Ingredients
2 Airline Chicken Breasts (About 8 Ounces Each)
6 Ounces Baby Purple Potatoes
3 Ounces Radishes, Without Greens (About 6 Radishes)
¼ Pound Snow Peas
3 Tablespoons Pistachios, Roasted & Salted
3-4 Sprigs Tarragon
1 Shallot
2 Tablespoons Sugar
1 Tablespoon Butter

1 Prepare the ingredients

Wash and dry the fresh produce. Heat a small pot of salted water to boiling on high. Remove the chicken from the refrigerator to bring to room temperature. Cut the potatoes and radishes into rounds. Snap off the stem of each snow pea and pull off the tough string that runs the length of the pod; cut each pod in half on an angle. Roughly chop the pistachios. Pick the tarragon leaves off the stems; discard the stems and finely chop the leaves. Peel and thinly slice the shallot.

2 Cook the potatoes

Add the potatoes to the pot of boiling water. Cook 7 to 9 minutes, or until tender when pierced with a fork. Drain thoroughly and set aside. Rinse and wipe out the pot.

3 Cook the chicken

While the potatoes cook, pat the chicken dry and season with salt and pepper on both sides. In a large pan (nonstick, if you have one), heat 2 teaspoons of olive oil on medium until hot. Add the seasoned chicken, skin side down first, and cook, loosely covering the pan with aluminum foil, 7 to 9 minutes per side, or until golden brown and cooked through. Transfer the cooked chicken to a plate, leaving any browned bits (or fond) in the pan. Loosely cover the plate with aluminum foil to keep warm.

4 Make the candied pistachios

While the chicken cooks, lightly grease a small sheet pan or line it with parchment paper. In the same pot used to cook the potatoes, heat the sugar and ¼ cup of water to boiling on medium-high, without stirring. Boil the sugar water 2 to 3 minutes, or just until it turns medium amber in color. Immediately remove the pot from heat and add the pistachios. Stir until thoroughly coated. Using a spoon or spatula, spread the candied nut mixture in an even layer on the prepared sheet pan. Set aside to cool.

5 Cook the vegetables & plate your dish

To the pan of reserved chicken fond, add 2 teaspoons of olive oil and heat on medium until hot. Add the drained potatoes and cook 1 to 2 minutes per side, or until lightly browned. Add the shallot; cook, stirring occasionally, 30 seconds to 1 minute, or until fragrant. Add the snow peas and radishes; season with salt and pepper. Cook, stirring occasionally, 1 to 2 minutes, or until slightly softened. Add the butter; stir until melted. Add the tarragon and remove from heat; season with salt and pepper to taste. To plate your dish, divide the cooked vegetables and chicken between 2 plates. Break apart the candied pistachios and place on top of each piece of chicken.

Salmon Roll Sandwiches
with Baby Beet & Pea Shoot Salad

Pea shoots are one the best and easiest ways to put a spring salad over the top. Their beauty, mild earthiness and slight crunch add brightness and texture to the ingredients around them. In fact, we think pea shoots are so great that we're making them a main salad ingredient. Served with cooked beet wedges, they make the perfect, healthful side for our take on the traditional New England seafood sandwich.

MAKES 2 SERVINGS · ABOUT 615 CALORIES PER SERVING

Ingredients

½ Pound Red Baby Beets, Without Greens
2 5-Ounce Skin-On Salmon Fillets
1 Small Bunch Chives
3-4 Sprigs Parsley
1 Lemon
1 Shallot
1 Stalk Celery
¼ Cup Mayonnaise
1 Tablespoon Red Wine Vinegar
1 Ounce Pea Shoots
2 Long Potato Rolls

1 Cook the beets

Heat a medium pot of salted water to boiling on high. Add the beets and cook 28 to 32 minutes, or until tender when pierced with a fork. Drain thoroughly and let stand until cool enough to handle. Using a paper towel and your fingers, gently rub the skin off each beet; discard the skins. Trim off and discard the top of each beet; cut each bulb into wedges and place in a medium bowl.

2 Prepare the ingredients

While the beets cook, wash and dry the fresh produce. Remove the salmon from the refrigerator to bring to room temperature. Finely chop the chives and parsley. Using a peeler, remove the yellow rind of the lemon, avoiding the white pith; mince the rind to get 2 teaspoons of zest. Quarter the lemon and remove the seeds. Peel and mince the shallot. Small dice the celery.

3 Make the salmon filling

While the beets continue to cook, pat the salmon fillets dry with paper towels and season with salt and pepper on both sides. In a medium pan (nonstick, if you have one), heat 2 teaspoons of olive oil on medium-high until hot. Add the seasoned salmon fillets, skin side down first, and cook, loosely covering the pan with aluminum foil, 3 to 5 minutes per side, or until cooked through. Transfer the cooked salmon to a plate and let rest. Wipe out the pan and set aside. When the salmon is cool enough to handle, remove and discard the skin. Using a fork or your hands, break the cooked salmon into large pieces and place in a large bowl. To the bowl of cooked salmon pieces, add the celery, lemon zest, chives, parsley, mayonnaise, half the shallot and the juice of 2 lemon wedges. Season with salt and pepper and gently mix until combined. Set aside.

4 Dress the beets & pea shoots

Add the vinegar and remaining shallot to the bowl of cooked beet wedges. Season with salt and pepper and drizzle with olive oil; toss until thoroughly combined. In a separate bowl, toss the pea shoots with a drizzle of olive oil and the juice of 1 lemon wedge (you will have an extra lemon wedge); season with salt and pepper.

5 Toast the rolls & plate your dish

In the same pan used to cook the salmon, heat 2 teaspoons of olive oil on medium-high until hot. Open the potato rolls and add them to the pan, interior side down; toast 30 seconds to 1 minute, or until lightly browned. Transfer to a plate. To plate your dish, fill each toasted potato roll with half the salmon mixture and divide between plates. Serve with the pea shoots and beets on the side.

Three Pea Salad
with Lemon Farro & Goat Cheese

We love fresh peas! And in spring, we get to revel in their delicate crunch and flavor. In this recipe, we're taking advantage of three different forms of the pea. We're using both the pea shoots, or the young, flavorful sprouts of the plant, and the ripe pods of snap peas and English peas. The latter two pea varieties are similar, but there are some general distinctions: snap peas are typically larger and milder, while English peas are more complex in taste and have a very short season. Together (pea shoots, too), they're delicious, especially when topped with silky goat cheese and tart lemon.

MAKES 2 SERVINGS • ABOUT 600 CALORIES PER SERVING

Ingredients

6 Ounces Sugar Snap Peas
½ Pound English Peas, With Shells
3 Ounces Pea Shoots
3 Radishes, Without Greens
4 Ounces Goat Cheese
4 Sprigs Mint
1 Lemon
¾ Cup Pearled Farro
3 Tablespoons Sunflower Seeds, Shelled & Raw
3 Ounces Arugula

1 Prepare the ingredients

Wash and dry the fresh produce. Heat 2 medium pots of salted water to boiling on high. Snap off the stem of each snap pea and pull off the tough string that runs the length of the pod. Shell the English peas. Trim off and discard the bottom inch of the pea shoot stems. Cut the radishes into thin rounds. Crumble the goat cheese into large pieces. Pick the mint leaves off the stems; discard the stems and finely chop the leaves. Using a peeler, remove the yellow rind of the lemon, avoiding the white pith; mince the rind to get 2 teaspoons of zest. Quarter the lemon and remove the seeds.

2 Cook the farro & make the vinaigrette

Add the farro and lemon zest to the first pot of boiling water. Cook 14 to 16 minutes, or until tender. Drain thoroughly and rinse under cold water to stop the cooking process. Set aside. While the farro cooks, squeeze the juice of 2 lemon wedges into a small bowl and season with salt and pepper. Slowly whisk in 2 tablespoons of olive oil until well combined. Set aside.

3 Blanch the peas

While the farro continues to cook, fill a medium bowl with ice water and set aside. Add the shelled English peas and snap peas to the second pot of boiling water and cook 30 seconds to 1 minute, or until bright green and slightly tender. Drain thoroughly and transfer to the bowl of ice water. Let stand until completely cooled, then drain thoroughly. Set aside.

4 Toast the sunflower seeds

Heat a small, dry pan on medium-high until hot. Add the sunflower seeds and toast, stirring frequently, 3 to 4 minutes, or until browned. Transfer to a small bowl and set aside.

5 Finish & plate your dish

In a large bowl, combine the cooked farro, drained peas, pea shoots, radishes, arugula, mint and toasted sunflower seeds; season with salt and pepper. Add enough vinaigrette to coat the greens (you may have extra vinaigrette); toss gently to mix. To plate your dish, divide the salad between 2 plates. Top with the goat cheese and garnish with the remaining lemon wedges.

Sesame Chicken
with Soba Noodles & Snap Peas

Soba is a traditional Japanese noodle dish, usually
served with dipping sauce on the side. But we made our
version with the sesame-peanut sauce built in—along
with a vegetable stir-fry featuring snap peas. Snap peas
add a wonderful crunch to tender soba noodles, made
with buckwheat flour. ("Soba" is the word for buckwheat
in Japanese.) In Japan, it's customary to loudly slurp
the noodles when eating them with chopsticks, a sign of
respect that also aerates the steaming noodles, cooling
them slightly. Feel free to do the same!

MAKES 2 SERVINGS · ABOUT 700 CALORIES PER SERVING

Ingredients

2 5-Ounce Boneless, Skinless Chicken Breasts
2 Cloves Garlic
1 1-Inch Piece Ginger
1 Carrot
¼ Pound Sugar Snap Peas
1 Bunch Cilantro
1 Lime
6 Ounces Soba Noodles
2 Tablespoons Soy Sauce
1 Tablespoon Sesame Oil
¼ Cup Creamy Peanut Butter
1 Teaspoon White Sesame Seeds

1 Prepare the ingredients

Wash and dry the fresh produce. Remove the chicken from the refrigerator to bring to room temperature. Heat a medium pot of salted water to boiling on high. Peel and mince the garlic and ginger. Peel the carrot and cut into thin sticks. Trim off and discard the ends the snap peas. Pick the cilantro leaves off the stems; discard the stems. Quarter the lime. Cut the chicken into bite-sized pieces.

2 Cook the noodles

Once the pot of water is boiling, add the soba noodles. Cook 4 to 6 minutes, or until tender. Drain thoroughly and rinse under cold water to prevent them from sticking together. Set aside.

3 Make the sauce

While the noodles cook, in a medium bowl, combine the soy sauce, sesame oil, peanut butter, the juice of 2 lime wedges and ¼ cup of water; whisk until well combined.

4 Cook the chicken

Pat the chicken dry with paper towels and season with salt and pepper. In a large pan (nonstick, if you have one), heat 2 teaspoons of oil on medium-high until hot. Add the seasoned chicken and cook, stirring occasionally, 3 to 4 minutes, or until lightly browned.

5 Finish & plate your dish

Add the garlic and ginger to the pan of chicken; reduce the heat to medium. Cook, stirring frequently, 30 to 45 seconds, or until fragrant. Add the carrot and snap peas; cook, stirring occasionally, 2 to 3 minutes, or until the vegetables are slightly tender and the chicken is cooked through. Stir in the sauce and cook, stirring occasionally, 30 to 45 seconds, or until heated through. Remove from heat. Rinse the cooked noodles once more under hot water to loosen them, then divide them between 2 bowls. Top with the chicken and vegetables. Garnish with the sesame seeds, cilantro and remaining lime wedges.

Homemade Ricotta Ravioli
with English Peas & Lemon Brown Butter

Making delicious, homemade ravioli is as simple as sealing fresh pasta sheets around a creamy ricotta cheese filling. To make it springier, we're finishing the ravioli with fresh peas in a brown butter sauce. By swirling the melted butter in a hot pan, you'll toast the milk solids. The butter goes from golden to amber brown, then becomes an irresistibly nutty and fragrant sauce. Adding lemon juice balances the butter's richness with the perfect amount of acidity.

MAKES 2 SERVINGS · ABOUT 680 CALORIES PER SERVING

Ingredients

4 Garlic Cloves
1 Shallot
4 Sprigs Mint
1 Lemon
½ Pound English Peas, With Shells
1 Cup Part-Skim Ricotta Cheese
⅓ Cup Grated Parmesan Cheese
1 Farm Egg
¼ Cup All-Purpose Flour
6 Fresh Pasta Sheets
2 Tablespoons Butter

1 Prepare the ingredients

Wash and dry the fresh produce. Heat a large pot of salted water to boiling on high. Peel and mince the garlic and shallot. Pick the mint leaves off the stems; discard the stems. Using a peeler, remove the yellow rind of the lemon, avoiding the white pith; mince the rind to get 2 teaspoons of zest. Quarter the lemon and remove the seeds. Shell the peas.

2 Make the filling

In a medium bowl, whisk together the ricotta cheese, Parmesan cheese, egg, lemon zest, half the mint (finely chopping before adding) and a drizzle of olive oil until smooth; season with salt and pepper.

3 Make the ravioli

Lightly dust a clean, dry work surface with some of the flour. Working one at a time, place a pasta sheet onto the floured work surface. Using a pastry brush or your fingers, lightly moisten the top of the pasta sheet with water. Spoon 3 dollops of filling (about 1 tablespoon each) onto one half of the moistened sheet, about 1½ inches apart. Fold the pasta sheet over the filling, then make 2 cuts in the pasta sheet between the dollops of filling to make 3 square ravioli. Gently press the edges together around each dollop to remove any air around the filling and to seal the filling within. Using a fork, firmly press the sealed edges of each ravioli to crimp and completely seal it. Set aside. (If your pasta sheets are sticking to the work surface, dust it with the remaining flour.)

4 Cook the aromatics

In a large pan (nonstick, if you have one), melt the butter with 1 teaspoon of olive oil on medium-high until hot; continue cooking until the butter foams. Once the foam subsides, over the heat, swirl the butter around the pan for 2 to 3 minutes, or until golden brown and nuttily fragrant. (Be careful, as the butter can burn easily.) Add the garlic and shallot and cook, stirring occasionally, 30 seconds to 1 minute, or until softened and fragrant. Remove from heat and stir in the juice of 2 lemon wedges. Set aside.

5 Cook the ravioli & finish your dish

Add the ravioli to the pot of boiling water and cook 3 to 5 minutes, or until cooked through. Reserve ½ cup of the pasta cooking water; using a slotted spoon or strainer, transfer the cooked ravioli to the pan of butter and aromatics. Add the peas and ¼ cup of the reserved pasta water; cook on medium heat, stirring occasionally, 2 to 4 minutes, or until well combined. (If the sauce seems dry, add the remaining reserved pasta water until you achieve your desired consistency.) Remove from heat. Season with salt and pepper to taste. Divide the ravioli and peas between 2 dishes. Garnish with the remaining mint and lemon wedges.

Sweet Miso Cod

with Snap Peas, Farro & Lime Beurre Blanc

Snap peas are the perfect side for tender, flaky cod. Their light, delicious crunch provides an incredible textural contrast. And their mild, seasonal flavor balances that of the traditional Japanese ingredients in this dish, from miso to soy to mirin. Beurre blanc sauce, or literally "white butter," is a French creation, and it's a terrific addition to the mix. The finished product, with earthy farro and the bite of citrus, is a complex-tasting meal that's fast and easy to make.

MAKES 2 SERVINGS • ABOUT 620 CALORIES PER SERVING

Ingredients

2 5-Ounce Cod Fillets
2 Tablespoons Soy Sauce
6 Ounces Sugar Snap Peas
3 Cloves Garlic
1 Lime
½ Cup Semi-Pearled Farro
1 Tablespoon Mirin
1 Tablespoon White Miso Paste
1 Tablespoon Granulated Sugar
2 Tablespoons Butter

1 Prepare the ingredients

Preheat the oven to 500°F. Wash and dry the fresh produce. Heat a medium pot of salted water to boiling on high. Place the cod in a shallow bowl or dish with the soy sauce; set aside to marinate. Trim off and discard the stems of the snap peas. Peel the garlic cloves. Mince 1 clove; smash with the side of your knife until it resembles a paste. Mince the remaining cloves. Cut the lime into 6 wedges.

2 Cook the farro

Add the farro to the pot of boiling water. Cook 16 to 18 minutes, or until tender. Drain thoroughly and return to the pot.

3 Roast the cod

While the farro cooks, in a small bowl, combine the garlic paste, mirin, miso paste and sugar; stir until thoroughly combined. Place the marinated cod on a lightly oiled sheet pan; spoon the mirin-miso mixture on top of each fillet. Roast in the oven 7 to 10 minutes, or until golden brown on top and cooked through.

4 Cook the snap peas

While the cod roasts, in a large pan, heat 2 teaspoons of olive oil on medium-high until hot. Add the minced garlic and snap peas; season with salt and pepper. Cook, stirring frequently, 1 to 2 minutes, or until the snap peas are bright green and slightly tender. Remove from heat. Divide the cooked snap peas between 2 plates.

5 Make the beurre blanc sauce & plate your dish

Off the heat, squeeze the juice of 4 lime wedges into the pan used to cook the snap peas. Add the butter and swirl the pan until the butter has just melted; season with salt and pepper to taste. Add 1 spoonful of the sauce to the cooked farro; stir to combine and season with salt and pepper to taste. Divide the dressed farro between the plates of snap peas. Top each with a roasted cod fillet. Spoon the remaining sauce over each plate. Garnish with the remaining lime wedges.

Lemon & Pea Tendril Risotto
with Saffron & Microgreens

We're so wild about pea tendrils, we're using them twice in this risotto. First, we're stirring them into the cooked risotto with Parmesan and butter, to soften them and incorporate them into the creamy rice grains. Next, we're using pea tendrils as a garnish, along with lemon and flavorful microgreens. The risotto itself is made with bomba rice, a Spanish variety. Usually reserved for paella, bomba is incredibly absorbent and keeps its shape. When cooking, remember: risotto is meant to be thick, creamy and al dente. Keep an eye on the risotto and taste it frequently to ensure that your rice is still slightly firm to the bite.

MAKES 2 SERVINGS • ABOUT 555 CALORIES PER SERVING

Ingredients
3 Cloves Garlic
2 Ounces Pea Tendrils
1 Lemon
1 Red Bell Pepper
1 Yellow Onion
1 Cup Bomba Rice
3 Tablespoons Vegetable Demi-Glace
1 Pinch Saffron
⅓ Cup Grated Parmesan Cheese
2 Tablespoons Butter
¼ Cup Microgreens

1 Prepare the ingredients

Wash and dry the fresh produce. Peel and mince the garlic. Roughly chop half the pea tendrils; leave the remaining pea tendrils whole. Using a peeler, remove the yellow rind of the lemon, avoiding the white pith; mince the rind to get 2 teaspoons of zest. Quarter the lemon and remove the seeds. Remove and discard the stem, seeds and ribs of the bell pepper; medium dice the pepper. Peel and small dice the onion.

2 Cook the aromatics & toast the rice

In a medium pot, heat 2 teaspoons of olive oil on medium until hot. Add the garlic and onion; season with salt and pepper. Cook, stirring frequently, 3 to 5 minutes, or until softened and fragrant. Add the bell pepper; season with salt and pepper. Cook, stirring frequently, 2 to 4 minutes, or until slightly softened. Increase the heat to medium-high and stir in the rice. Cook, stirring frequently, 1 to 2 minutes, or until toasted and fragrant.

3 Start the risotto

Stir the vegetable demi-glace, saffron, lemon zest, the juice of 1 lemon wedge and 3½ cups of water into the pan of aromatics and rice; season with salt and pepper. Bring the mixture to a boil. Once boiling, reduce the heat to medium-low and simmer, stirring occasionally, 14 to 16 minutes, or until most of the liquid has been absorbed and the rice is al dente (still slightly firm to the bite). Remove from heat.

4 Finish the risotto

Off the heat, stir the Parmesan cheese, chopped pea tendrils and butter into the risotto; season with salt and pepper to taste.

5 Dress the tendrils & plate your dish

Just before serving, in a medium bowl, dress the whole pea tendrils with the juice of 1 lemon wedge and 1 teaspoon of olive oil; season with salt and pepper. To plate your dish, divide the risotto between 2 bowls and top with the dressed pea tendrils. Garnish with the microgreens and remaining lemon wedges.

Salmon & Whole Wheat Israeli Couscous
with Fava Bean-Olive Relish

Served with fava beans, this dish is a delicious hello to spring. What started as a staple substitute has become a delicacy. Israeli couscous (also known as "ptitim") was originally produced to combat rice shortages in Israel in the 1950s. Made from hardy wheat that's been rolled into balls and toasted, these little pearls have an incredible, smoky depth of flavor. Fava beans, olives and chives make the perfect zesty relish.

MAKES 2 SERVINGS • ABOUT 615 CALORIES PER SERVING

Ingredients
2 5-Ounce Skin-On Salmon Fillets
2 Cloves Garlic
8-10 Castelvetrano Olives
1 Carrot
1 Yellow Onion
1 Small Bunch Chives
2 Sprigs Dill
1 Lemon
½ Pound Fresh Fava Beans, In Shells
1 Cup Whole Wheat Israeli Couscous

1 Prepare the ingredients

Wash and dry the fresh produce. Heat 2 pots of salted water to boiling on high. Remove the salmon from the refrigerator to bring to room temperature. Peel and mince the garlic. Using the side of your knife, smash the olives; remove and discard the pits. Roughly chop the olives. Peel and small dice the carrot and onion. Mince the chives. Roughly chop the dill. Using a peeler, remove the yellow rind of the lemon, avoiding the white pith; mince the rind to get 2 teaspoons of zest. Quarter the lemon and remove the seeds. Shell the fava beans; discard the shells.

2 Cook the couscous

Add the couscous to the first pot of boiling water. Cook 5 to 7 minutes, or until tender and cooked through. Drain thoroughly and rinse under cold water for 30 seconds to 1 minute to stop the cooking process. Return the cooked couscous to the pot and set aside.

3 Make the fava bean relish

Add the fava beans to the second pot of boiling water. Cook 30 seconds to 1 minute, or until slightly softened. Drain thoroughly; place in a bowl of ice water to stop the cooking process. Working one at a time, using your fingertips, remove each bean from the bowl of ice water. Break off the tip of each bean and squeeze it out of its outer skin; discard the skin and set the bean aside. Repeat with the remaining beans. In a medium bowl, combine the peeled fava beans, olives, lemon zest, chives and 2 teaspoons of olive oil. Season with salt and pepper to taste. Set aside.

4 Cook the salmon

Season the salmon fillets with salt and pepper on both sides. In a medium pan (nonstick, if you have one), heat 2 teaspoons of olive oil on medium until hot. Add the seasoned fillets and cook, loosely covering the pan with aluminum foil, 3 to 4 minutes per side, or until cooked through. Transfer to a plate and set aside in a warm place. Wipe out the pan.

5 Finish the couscous & plate your dish

In the same pan used to cook the salmon, heat 2 teaspoons of olive oil on medium until hot. Add the onion, garlic and carrot; season with salt and pepper. Cook, stirring occasionally, 3 to 4 minutes, or until softened. Add the cooked couscous, dill and the juice of 2 lemon wedges. Cook, stirring occasionally, 1 to 2 minutes, or until warmed through. To plate your dish, divide the couscous between 2 plates. Top each with a cooked salmon fillet and the fava bean relish. Garnish with the remaining lemon wedges.

Spring Minestrone
with Fresh Fava Beans & Asparagus

Fava beans are one of the oldest crops known to man, with evidence of cultivation dating back more than seven millennia. Many Italians believe that fava beans actually saved the population of Sicily from starvation in the Middle Ages, when all other crops failed. Some even continue to carry fava beans around with them wherever they go, as good luck charms. In this recipe, fresh, blanched fava beans complete our take on traditional minestrone. We're also cooking the pasta in the soup's zesty tomato broth and flavoring it with asparagus and Parmesan cheese.

MAKES 2 SERVINGS • ABOUT 580 CALORIES PER SERVING

Ingredients

3 Cloves Garlic
2 Stalks Celery
3-4 Sprigs Parsley
1 Carrot
1 Yellow Onion
1 Lemon
½ Pound Asparagus
½ Pound Fresh Fava Beans, In Shells
1 Cup Vegetable Broth
1 15-Ounce Can Diced Tomatoes
6 Ounces Dried Ditalini Pasta
⅓ Cup Grated Parmesan Cheese

1 Prepare the ingredients

Wash and dry the fresh produce. Heat a small pot of water to boiling on high. Peel and thinly slice the garlic. Small dice the celery. Pick the parsley leaves off the stems; discard the stems. Peel and small dice the carrot and onion. Using a peeler, remove the yellow rind of the lemon, avoiding the white pith; mince the rind to get 2 teaspoons of zest. Quarter the lemon and remove the seeds. Snap off and discard the woody ends of the asparagus; cut the asparagus into 1-inch pieces on an angle. Shell the fava beans; discard the shells.

2 Cook the aromatics

In a medium pot, heat 2 teaspoons of olive oil on medium until hot. Add the garlic, carrot, celery and onion; season with salt and pepper. Cook, stirring occasionally, 3 to 5 minutes, or until softened.

3 Make the soup

Stir the vegetable broth, lemon zest, tomatoes and 3 cups of water into the pot of vegetables. Season with salt and pepper. Bring to a boil on high. Once boiling, reduce the heat to medium-low and simmer 4 to 6 minutes, or until slightly reduced in volume.

4 Blanch the fava beans

While the soup simmers, add the fava beans to the small pot of boiling water. Cook 30 seconds to 1 minute, or until slightly softened. Drain thoroughly; place in a bowl of ice water to stop the cooking process. Working one at a time, using your fingertips, remove each bean from the bowl of ice water. Break off the tip of each bean and squeeze it out of its outer skin; discard the skin and set the bean aside. Repeat with the remaining beans.

5 Add the pasta & asparagus

Add the pasta to the pot of soup and cook 10 to 12 minutes, or until the pasta is al dente (still slightly firm to the bite). Add the asparagus, half the Parmesan cheese and half the parsley (roughly chopping before adding). Season with salt and pepper. Cook, stirring occasionally, 1 to 2 minutes, or until the asparagus is bright green and the Parmesan cheese is thoroughly incorporated. Remove from heat. Stir in the juice of 2 lemon wedges. To plate your dish, divide the soup between 2 bowls and top each with the peeled fava beans. Garnish with the remaining parsley, Parmesan cheese and lemon wedges.

Artichokes

FIELD GUIDE TO ARTICHOKES

The following are some of our favorite heirloom and specialty varieties. The best place to find them is at your local farmers' market, or you can grow them. The seeds are available at seed saver websites.

Green Globe: Available year-round, but peak harvest happens in spring. Has been known to botanists and eaten for at least 2,000 years. A member of the thistle family.

Opera Artichoke: First grown in Southern Italy by botanists trying to ensure higher yields. The result was a large, delicate globe-shaped artichoke with a subtle, nutty flavor.

Purple of Romagna Artichoke: An exceptionally tender purple variety. Grows best in warmer areas. Native to Northeastern Italy.

Violet de Provence Artichoke: Heirloom variety from Southern France. Tightly packed, globular and purple-leaved heads. As one of the older cultivars, is the parent plant for many smaller purple artichokes.

Violetta Precoce Artichoke: A pointed, purple variety native to Northern Italy. Grows without spines or thorns. Named for its quick maturation period. Harvested early in the season.

IF ARTICHOKES HAVE ever looked slightly, well, *dangerous* to you, there's a reason! They're a relative of the thistle—the wild, spiky plant that makes it hard to walk barefoot in fields and interrupts the grazing of farm animals. In fact, the wrapped, green leaves, or "bracts," of the vegetable are simply prickly spines bred over the centuries to be wide, fleshy and delicious.

It's because of this bristling gene pool (designed to keep herbivorous animals away) that only two parts of the artichoke are edible: the pad-like bases of the bracts (usually dipped in melted butter or sauce and scraped off with the front teeth) and the tender, flavorful "heart," located just under the rough, inedible "choke"—a clustered mass of purplish, premature buds.

For the artichoke, like the thistle, is a flower. If allowed to mature, its bracts curl outward, revealing a crown of stunning blue florets. The vegetable is harvested just before that moment, when the green globes hang heavy on the stems, and all of those unspent nutrients are concentrated in the interior.

Artichokes are usually boiled or steamed, after the fibrous, thorny parts of the bracts have been removed. Stuffed artichoke recipes are also popular the world over. Picked in spring, this hearty, delicious "thistle" is friendly to our taste buds, with its rich tones of earthy succulence.

Chicken, Baby Artichoke & Spinach Casserole
with Gouda Béchamel

Baby artichokes are a wonderful spring ingredient. They aren't a separate variety. They're simply artichokes that are smaller when fully mature. And most amazing: they don't develop the coarse part of the "choke" in the center of the plant (the fuzzy beginnings of the artichoke's beautiful, purplish-blue flower). As a result, they're almost fully edible, though they do still require a little trimming. In this chicken casserole, their freshness cuts the rich creaminess of the Gouda cheese béchamel sauce.

MAKES 2 SERVINGS • ABOUT 695 CALORIES PER SERVING

Ingredients
2 6-Ounce Boneless, Skinless Chicken Breasts
2 Ounces Baby Spinach
2 Cloves Garlic
2 Ounces Gouda Cheese
3-4 Sprigs Parsley
1 Yellow Onion
4 Baby Artichokes (About 10 Ounces)
2 Ounces Wide, Curly Egg Noodles
1 Tablespoon White Wine Vinegar
2 Tablespoons Butter
3 Tablespoons All-Purpose Flour
1 Cup Low-Fat Milk
1 Teaspoon Hungarian Paprika
¼ Cup Grated Parmesan Cheese
¼ Cup Panko Breadcrumbs

1 Prepare the ingredients

Preheat the oven to 375°F. Wash and dry the fresh produce. Remove the chicken from the refrigerator to bring to room temperature. Heat a medium pot of salted water to boiling on high. Roughly chop the spinach. Peel and mince the garlic. Grate the Gouda cheese. Pick the parsley leaves off the stems; discard the stems and roughly chop the leaves. Peel and small dice the onion. Cut the chicken breasts into bite-sized pieces.

2 Prepare the baby artichokes

Trim off and discard the tips of the artichoke stems. Trim off and discard 1 inch from the tops of the artichokes (to remove the sharp tops). Peel off and discard the outer leaves until you reach the tender, middle leaves. Using a paring knife, cut off and discard the outer skins of the stems. Halve the artichokes lengthwise and add to a bowl of cold water along with the vinegar.

3 Cook the pasta & sauté the chicken & vegetables

Once the water is boiling, add the noodles; cook 3 to 4 minutes, or until just shy of al dente. Remove from heat. Reserve ¼ cup of pasta water; drain the noodles thoroughly. Transfer to a bowl. Wipe out the pot. While the pasta cooks, season the chicken with salt and pepper on all sides. In a large pan, heat 2 teaspoons of olive oil on medium-high until hot. Add the chicken; cook 2 to 3 minutes. Add the artichokes and onions. Cook, stirring frequently, 2 to 3 minutes, or until the onions have softened and the chicken is cooked through. Season with salt and pepper to taste.

4 Make the béchamel sauce

In the same pot used to cook the pasta, melt the butter on medium. Add the garlic and cook, stirring frequently, 30 seconds to 1 minute, or until fragrant. Add the flour; cook, stirring constantly, 30 seconds to 1 minute, or until golden. Slowly add the milk, whisking constantly, until thoroughly combined and no lumps remain. Bring the mixture to a boil. Once boiling, reduce the heat to low; simmer, whisking constantly, 3 to 4 minutes, or until thickened. Add the spinach, paprika, Gouda cheese and Parmesan cheese. Whisk until thoroughly incorporated. Remove from heat. Season with salt and pepper to taste.

5 Bake the casserole

To the pot of béchamel, add the chicken and vegetables. Rinse the noodles under cold water to loosen them, then add them to the pot; stir to combine. (If the sauce seems dry, add up to ¼ cup of the reserved pasta water to achieve your desired consistency.) Transfer to a baking dish. In a bowl, toss the breadcrumbs with a drizzle of olive oil; evenly sprinkle over the casserole. Bake 8 to 10 minutes, or until golden brown. Remove from the oven. Let stand for 2 minutes before serving. Garnish with the parsley.

Baby Artichoke Risotto
with Shiitake Mushrooms, Mustard Greens & Goat Cheese

In this dish, we're using the earthiness of baby artichokes (small, mature artichokes) to add natural richness to risotto. Risotto gets its luxurious, creamy texture not from milk or cream, but from starches in the rice released as the grains are heated. Artichoke, with its delicious, succulent flesh, makes the perfect pairing. And for a bright, tangy note, we're adding goat cheese. The result is a dish that's bursting with flavor.

MAKES 2 SERVINGS • ABOUT 680 CALORIES PER SERVING

Ingredients

4 Ounces Shiitake Mushrooms
3 Cloves Garlic
1 Small Bunch Chives
1 Yellow Onion
½ Pound Mustard Greens
1 Lemon
6 Ounces Baby Artichokes (About 5)
1 Cup Arborio Rice
1 Cup Vegetable Broth
2 Ounces Goat Cheese
¼ Cup Grated Parmesan Cheese

1 Prepare the ingredients

Wash and dry the fresh produce. Remove and discard the mushroom stems; thinly slice the caps. Peel and finely chop the garlic. Cut the chives into ¼-inch pieces. Peel and small dice the onion. Remove and discard the stems of the mustard greens; chop the leaves into bite-sized pieces. Halve the lemon and remove the seeds.

2 Prepare the artichokes

Trim off and discard the tips of the baby artichoke stems. Trim off and discard 1 inch from the tops of the baby artichokes (to remove the sharp points). Peel off and discard the tough, outer leaves until you reach the tender, middle leaves. Using a paring knife, cut off and discard the outer skins of the stems. Halve the baby artichokes lengthwise and add to a bowl of cold water along with the juice of 1 lemon half.

3 Cook the vegetables

In a medium pot, heat 2 teaspoons of olive oil on medium-high until hot. Add the mushrooms and cook, stirring occasionally, 1 to 3 minutes, or until slightly browned. Add the onion and garlic; season with salt and pepper. Cook, stirring frequently, 1 to 2 minutes, or until slightly softened.

4 Make the risotto

Stir the arborio rice into the pot of vegetables. Cook, stirring frequently, 30 seconds to 1 minute, or until toasted and fragrant. Add the vegetable broth and 1 cup of water. Bring the mixture to a boil, then reduce the heat to medium-low; simmer, stirring frequently, 5 to 7 minutes. Add another ½ cup of water and stir in the mustard greens; cook 1 to 2 minutes, or until wilted. Add the baby artichokes; cook, stirring frequently, 9 to 11 minutes, or until the rice is cooked through. (If the rice seems dry during cooking, add another ½ cup of water to the pot.) Season with salt and pepper to taste.

5 Finish & plate your dish

Stir the goat cheese and half the Parmesan cheese into the pot of risotto; season with salt and pepper to taste. To plate your dish, divide the risotto between 2 bowls. Cut the remaining lemon half into wedges. Garnish the risotto with the chives, lemon wedges and remaining Parmesan cheese.

East of the Pacific: Ocean Mist Farms

IN 1924, JUST south of Castroville, in California's fertile Salinas Valley, four families went into business together. Their office: a wood and tin shed. Their business: artichoke growing.

That modest enterprise has since grown into the most extraordinary artichoke farm in America.

Ocean Mist Farms, now its tenth decade, is a model of high-quality agriculture. Still owned and operated by the descendants of its five founders (two of whom were brothers), it has since grown to include other families, and other vegetables. But artichoke growing remains at the delectable heart of what makes Ocean Mist Farms so exceptional.

"At Ocean Mist Farms," says Chris Drew, the farm's Production Manager, "we want to be involved in every part of the experience of growing and preparing the world's best produce."

Ocean Mist Farms is more than a farm; it's a learning center. Its employees share their favorite recipes and cooking techniques for artichokes, which they lovingly call those "thorny, odd-looking little vegetables."

With the Pacific Ocean stretching just to the west, Ocean Mist's name isn't fanciful. When the wind is blowing, cool, salty mist actually blows up over the cliffs, settling atop the rows of furrowed soil.

Is that why their artichokes are so delicious?

Chris laughs. "Maybe," he says. "You never know."

Chicken, Mushroom & Baby Artichoke Stew
with Goat Cheese Polenta

Meet your new spring favorite. This warming chicken and vegetable stew on a bed of creamy polenta is perfect for the transition away from the cold season. At the heart of this dish is the pairing of artichokes with delicate oyster mushrooms. Named for their resemblance to fanned, rippling oyster shells, oyster mushrooms grow wild on tree bark in the primeval woods of Central Europe. In this dish, their fine, earthy taste brings out umami notes in the baby artichokes, lending complexity to the smooth, rich polenta.

MAKES 2 SERVINGS • ABOUT 700 CALORIES PER SERVING

Ingredients

2 Cloves Garlic
1 Lemon
1 Scallion
½ Pound Oyster Mushrooms
4 Sprigs Mint
½ Pound Baby Artichokes
¾ Cup Polenta
4 Ounces Goat Cheese
10 Ounces Ground Chicken
3 Tablespoons Chicken Demi-Glace
2 Tablespoons Butter

1 Prepare the ingredients

Wash and dry the fresh produce. In a medium pot, heat 3½ cups of salted water to boiling on high. Peel and thinly slice the garlic. Using a peeler, remove the yellow rind of the lemon, avoiding the white pith; mince the rind to get 2 teaspoons of zest. Quarter the lemon and remove the seeds. Cut off and discard the root end of the scallion; thinly slice the scallion on an angle, separating the white bottom and green top. Trim off the ends of the mushrooms. Pick the mint leaves off the stems; discard the stems.

2 Prepare the baby artichokes

Trim off and discard the tips of the baby artichoke stems. Trim off and discard 1 inch from the tops of the baby artichokes (to remove the sharp points). Peel off and discard the tough, outer leaves until you reach the tender, middle leaves. Using a paring knife, cut off and discard the outer skins of the stems. Halve the baby artichokes lengthwise and add to a bowl of cold water along with the juice of 2 lemon wedges.

3 Cook the polenta

Slowly stir the polenta and lemon zest into the pot of boiling water; continue stirring until no lumps remain. Reduce the heat to low and simmer, stirring frequently, 10 to 12 minutes, or until tender and thickened. Remove from heat and stir in the goat cheese; season with salt and pepper to taste. Set aside in a warm place.

4 Cook the chicken

While the polenta cooks, in a medium pan, heat 2 teaspoons of olive oil on medium-high until hot. Add the ground chicken; season with salt and pepper. Cook, frequently breaking the meat apart with a spoon, 4 to 5 minutes, or until cooked through. Transfer the cooked chicken to a plate and set aside. Wipe out the pan.

5 Cook the vegetables & plate your dish

In the same pan used to cook the chicken, heat 2 teaspoons of olive oil on medium-high until hot. Add the mushrooms and baby artichokes; season with salt and pepper. Cook, stirring occasionally, 3 to 4 minutes, or until browned and crispy. Add the white bottoms of the scallion; cook, stirring frequently, 30 seconds to 1 minute, or until fragrant. Add the chicken demi-glace and ½ cup of water; season with salt and pepper. Cook, stirring occasionally, 30 seconds to 1 minute, or until thoroughly combined. Add the butter and cooked chicken. Cook, stirring constantly, 1 to 2 minutes, or until thoroughly combined and the butter is completely melted; season with salt and pepper to taste. To plate your dish, divide the polenta between 2 dishes and top with the chicken-mushroom-baby artichoke stew. Garnish with the green tops of the scallion and mint. Serve with the remaining lemon wedges.

Strawberries & Rhubarb

FIELD GUIDE TO STRAWBERRIES & RHUBARB

The following are some of our favorite heirloom and specialty varieties. The best place to find them is at your local farmers' market, or you can grow them. The seeds are available at seed saver websites.

Fraise des Bois: Also known as the Alpine or woodland strawberry. This wild strawberry has been consumed by humans since the Stone Age. First cultivated in Persia and spread west along trade routes.

Glaskins Perpetual Rhubarb: First grown in Brighton, England, as a garden variety. Unlike many varieties, light cutting and early planting allow it to be harvested almost year-round.

Pineberries: A hybrid of North American and South American varieties. Easily recognized by its white color. Has a flavor reminiscent of pineapple, leading to its name.

Tristar Strawberries: Self-pollinating and cold resistant. Dubbed "everbearing" because it produces fruit year-round. Heaviest, best harvest happens in springtime. Championed for its deliciously sweet flavor.

Victoria Rhubarb: The "gold standard" of rhubarb. Thick, tart stalks prized by gardeners the world over. The variety hasn't been improved upon in 175 years—evidence of its superiority.

Yellow Wonder Wild Strawberries: A small, yellow-fruited variety of the European wild strawberry. Has a fine flavor. The farther north it is planted, the longer the harvest.

IN THIS CHAPTER, we're exploring two traditional springtime ingredients: rhubarb and strawberries. While we might be used to seeing them paired together and baked into buttery crusts, we think they deserve a place at the dinner table, too. In the recipes that follow, you'll enjoy them in a variety of ways, as an accent for savory dishes.

Rhubarb is decidedly spring. It's one of the first food plants harvested. Wild rhubarb is native to Asia, but it spread quickly and can now be found in cooler climates around the world. The crisp stalks have a pleasantly tart flavor and an almost lemony brightness. Though most of the world considers it a vegetable, in 1947, a New York court decided that,

because of how it was used, rhubarb was a fruit. (By law, it's still considered one.)

The strawberry has both European and American wild varieties. They'd been cultivated in Europe since about the 1400s, but development had stagnated by the Colonial period. Europeans discovered two distinct varieties of wild strawberry growing in North and South America. They were brought back to France, where they were planted and eventually hybridized, creating the strawberries we know today. These juicy morsels have a variety of uses. Fresh or cooked, they add a unique tang and provide a sweet counterpoint in all kinds of dishes.

Seared Flank Steak
with Crispy Shallots & Spinach-Strawberry Salad

This classic salad, a favorite of youngsters and seasoned chefs alike, is the perfect accompaniment for seared steaks. The naturally sweet tanginess of the strawberries adds brightness and punch to the spinach, earthy almonds, kohlrabi and ricotta salata cheese. The shallot vinaigrette that coats the salad rhymes in flavor with the crispy shallots that rest atop the dish. But strawberries are really what brings all of the elements together. They're the perfect springtime salad ingredient.

MAKES 2 SERVINGS • ABOUT 700 CALORIES PER SERVING

Ingredients

2 5-Ounce Flank Steaks
6 Ounces Strawberries
3 Tablespoons Almonds, Whole & Raw
2 Shallots
1 Tablespoon Balsamic Vinegar
1 Kohlrabi, Without Greens
2 Ounces Ricotta Salata Cheese
½ Pound Loose Spinach
½ Cup Rice Flour

1 Prepare the ingredients

Wash and dry the fresh produce. Remove the steaks from the refrigerator to bring to room temperature. Cut off and discard the tops of the strawberries; thinly slice the strawberries. Roughly chop the almonds. Peel the shallots. Thinly slice one shallot into rings; mince the remaining shallot and place in a small bowl with the balsamic vinegar. Peel the kohlrabi and cut into thin matchsticks. Crumble the ricotta salata cheese. Trim off and discard the stem ends of the spinach; tear the leaves into bite-sized pieces.

2 Cook the steaks

Pat the steaks dry with paper towels and season with salt and pepper on both sides. In a large pan, heat 2 teaspoons of olive oil on medium-high until hot. Add the seasoned steaks and cook 3 to 5 minutes per side, or until they reach your desired degree of doneness. Transfer the cooked steaks to a plate or cutting board and lightly cover with aluminum foil to keep warm. Set aside in a warm place and let rest for at least 5 minutes. Wipe out the pan.

3 Make the vinaigrette & toast the almonds

While the steaks cook, season the shallot-vinegar mixture with salt and pepper to taste. Slowly whisk in 2 tablespoons of olive oil until well combined; set aside. Once the steaks have finished cooking, heat the same pan used to cook them on medium until hot. Add the almonds and cook, stirring occasionally, 2 to 4 minutes, or until lightly browned and fragrant. Transfer to a small bowl and set aside. Wipe out the pan.

4 Cook the shallots

While the steaks continue to rest, in a medium bowl, whisk together the rice flour and ½ cup of water to create a thin batter. (As the batter stands, it may thicken. You may need to add up to ¼ cup of additional water to maintain a thin consistency.) Separate the shallot rings and add them to the batter; stir to thoroughly coat. In the same pan used to toast the almonds, heat a ¼-inch layer of oil on medium until hot. Using tongs or a fork, transfer the coated shallots (letting the excess batter drip off) to the pan in a single layer. (If necessary, work in batches to avoid over-crowding.) Cook 1 to 2 minutes, or until golden brown. Transfer to a paper towel-lined plate and immediately season with salt.

5 Finish & plate your dish

Find the lines of muscle (or grain) of the steaks. Slice the steaks crosswise, against the grain. In a large bowl, combine the spinach, kohlrabi, toasted almonds, ricotta salata cheese and strawberries. Add enough vinaigrette (you may have extra) to coat the greens; toss to mix and season with salt and pepper to taste. Divide the salad and sliced steak between 2 plates. Top each with the crispy shallots.

Grilled Brie Cheese Sandwiches
with Quick Strawberry Jam & Red Walnut-Arugula Salad

We love fruit preserves. But here's a little-known secret: they don't have to be preserved! Stewing fruits like strawberries with sugar releases their pectin, a natural preservative, but the jam is just as delicious when served right away. In this recipe, we give you a quick version of strawberry jam in our spin on the grilled cheese sandwich, made with soft, mild, delicious brie.

MAKES 2 SERVINGS • ABOUT 645 CALORIES PER SERVING

Ingredients

4 Ounces Brie Cheese
6 Ounces Strawberries
1 Lemon
3 Tablespoons Red Walnuts, Shelled & Raw
⅓ Cup Sugar
1 Tablespoon Whole Grain Dijon Mustard
1 Tablespoon Balsamic Vinegar
4 Slices 7-Grain Sandwich Bread
2 Tablespoons Butter
3 Ounces Arugula

1 Prepare the ingredients

Wash and dry the fresh produce. Thinly slice the brie cheese. Remove and discard the stems of the strawberries; medium dice the strawberries. Using a peeler, remove the yellow rind of the lemon, avoiding the white pith; mince the rind to get 2 teaspoons of zest. Quarter the lemon and remove the seeds. Roughly chop the walnuts.

2 Make the quick strawberry jam & balsamic dressing

In a medium pot, combine the strawberries, sugar, lemon zest, the juice of all 4 lemon wedges and a big pinch of salt. Cook, stirring occasionally, 10 to 12 minutes, or until thickened and syrupy. Transfer the quick strawberry jam to a plate and spread into a thin layer. Set aside to cool. While the strawberry jam cooks, in a small bowl, combine the mustard and vinegar; season with salt and pepper to taste. Slowly whisk in 2 tablespoons of olive oil until thoroughly combined. Set aside.

3 Toast the walnuts

While the strawberries continue to cook, heat a medium pan (nonstick, if you have one) on medium until hot. Add the walnuts and cook, stirring frequently, 2 to 3 minutes, or until lightly browned and fragrant. Transfer to a bowl. Wipe out the pan.

4 Assemble & cook the sandwiches

Lay 2 of the bread slices on a clean, dry work surface. Divide the brie cheese between the bread slices and top with the cooled strawberry jam; season with salt and pepper. Top with the remaining bread slices. In the same pan used to toast the walnuts, melt half the butter on medium heat until hot. Add the sandwiches and cook 2 to 3 minutes on the first side, or until golden brown and crispy. Using a spatula, carefully flip the sandwiches and add the remaining butter to the pan. Cook 2 to 3 minutes, or until the cheese has melted. Transfer to a cutting board.

5 Dress the salad & plate your dish

In a large bowl, combine the arugula, toasted walnuts and as much of the balsamic dressing as you'd like. Toss gently to coat and season with salt and pepper to taste. Cut the sandwiches in half and divide between 2 plates. Serve with the salad on the side.

Sliced Pork Steak
with Smashed Potatoes & Strawberry-Rhubarb Compote

In French, the word "compote" simply means "mixture," but the dish that goes by the same name is a mixture of a special kind. Fruit and spices are stewed together, resulting in a syrupy sauce that's usually served as a dessert. But it also makes a wonderful topping or marinade for savory ingredients—like these pork steaks, which we're serving with a spring compote of strawberry and rhubarb. Steak, a term usually used to describe beefsteak, can actually refer to many different types of meat (and these days, even to certain cauliflower and mushroom preparations). The Old Norse word "steikja" simply described a large cut of meat. The pork steaks in this recipe are cut from a roast that's been browned and finished in the oven.

MAKES 2 SERVINGS • ABOUT 610 CALORIES PER SERVING

Ingredients

¾ Pound Small Yukon Gold Potatoes
5 Ounces Strawberries
5 Ounces Spinach
4 Ounces Rhubarb
3 Scallions
1 Lemon
5-6 Castelvetrano Olives, With Pits
¼ Cup Crème Fraîche
1 10-Ounce Pork Roast
¼ Teaspoon Dried Orange Peel
¼ Teaspoon Ground Cardamom
⅛ Teaspoon Fennel Seeds

1   Prepare the ingredients

Preheat the oven to 450°F. Wash and dry the fresh produce. Heat a medium pot of salted water to boiling on high. Quarter the potatoes. Remove and discard the stems of the strawberries; small dice the strawberries. Small dice the rhubarb. Remove and discard the root ends of the scallions; thinly slice, separating the white bottoms and green tops. Using a peeler, remove the rind of the lemon, avoiding the white pith; mince the rind to get 2 teaspoons of zest. Quarter and deseed the lemon. Remove and discard the pits of the olives; roughly chop the olives.

2   Cook the potatoes

Add the potatoes to the pot of boiling water. Cook 9 to 11 minutes, or until tender when pierced with a fork. Drain thoroughly and return to the pot. Stir in the olives, crème fraîche, half the green tops of the scallions, half the lemon zest and the juice of 2 lemon wedges. Drizzle with olive oil and season with salt and pepper to taste.

3   Brown & roast the pork

While the potatoes cook, in a medium pan (nonstick, if you have one) heat 2 teaspoons of olive oil on medium-high until hot. Season the pork on all sides with salt and pepper. Add the pork to the pan and cook 3 to 5 minutes per side, or until evenly browned. Transfer to a high-sided sheet pan, leaving any browned bits (or fond) in the pan. Roast the browned pork in the oven 6 to 8 minutes, or until cooked to your desired degree of doneness. Remove from the oven and transfer to a plate or cutting board. Loosely cover with aluminum foil. Let rest for 5 minutes.

4   Cook the compote

While the pork roasts, in a medium pan (nonstick, if you have one), heat 1 teaspoon of olive oil on medium-high until hot. Add the dried orange peel, cardamom and fennel seeds. Cook, stirring frequently, 30 seconds to 1 minute, or until toasted and fragrant. Add the strawberries, rhubarb, the juice of the remaining lemon wedges and a pinch of salt; stir to thoroughly combine. Cook, stirring occasionally, 5 to 7 minutes, or until the strawberries and rhubarb are softened and stewed. Remove from heat and transfer to a bowl; set aside. Rinse and wipe out the pan.

5   Cook the spinach & plate your dish

While the pork rests, in the pan used to cook the compote, heat 1 teaspoon of olive oil on medium until hot. Add the white bottoms of the scallions and remaining lemon zest. Cook, stirring constantly, 30 seconds to 1 minute, or until fragrant. Add the spinach and cook, stirring frequently, 1 to 2 minutes, or until bright green and wilted. Remove from the heat and season with salt and pepper to taste. To plate your dish, slice the pork crosswise and divide between 2 dishes. Serve with the sautéed spinach, smashed potatoes and strawberry-rhubarb compote on the side. Garnish with the remaining green tops of the scallions.

Hearty Spring Salad
with Poached Chicken, Pickled Rhubarb & New Potatoes

In this recipe, you'll be taking one of our springtime
favorites—rhubarb—and highlighting its natural
tartness by quickly pickling it. The zesty pickles add
tang and accent the tarragon-infused poached chicken.
With a hearty, crisp salad of butter lettuce and
asparagus, this dish is as light and bright as the season
itself.

MAKES 2 SERVINGS · ABOUT 550 CALORIES PER SERVING

Ingredients
2 6-Ounce Boneless, Skinless Chicken Breasts
4 Ounces Easter Egg Radishes, Without Greens
4 Ounces Rhubarb
4 Ounces Asparagus
1 Head Butter Lettuce
6-8 Sprigs Tarragon
4 Ounces Goat Cheese
6 Ounces New Potatoes
2 Tablespoons Red Wine Vinegar
2 Tablespoons Granulated Sugar
1 Tablespoon Whole Grain Dijon Mustard
2 Teaspoons Poppy Seeds

1 Prepare the ingredients

Wash and dry the fresh produce. Heat a pot of salted water to boiling on high. Remove the chicken from the refrigerator to bring to room temperature. Cut the radishes into ½-inch wedges. Using a peeler, peel the rhubarb lengthwise into thin ribbons and transfer to a heatproof bowl. Trim off and discard the woody stems of the asparagus; cut the asparagus into 1-inch pieces on an angle. Cut out and discard the root of the lettuce; separate the leaves. Pick the tarragon leaves off the stems; reserve the stems and roughly chop the leaves. Crumble the goat cheese.

2 Cook the potatoes & asparagus

Place the potatoes in a medium pot and cover with cold water. Season with salt and heat to boiling on high. Once the water is boiling, cook the potatoes 13 to 15 minutes, or until tender when pierced with a fork. Add the asparagus; cook 2 to 3 minutes, or until bright green and tender. Drain thoroughly and transfer to a bowl. Using a fork, smash the potatoes. Drizzle with olive oil and season with salt and pepper to taste; stir thoroughly to coat. Set aside.

3 Cook the chicken

While the potatoes and asparagus cook, add the chicken and tarragon stems to the boiling water. Cook 8 to 10 minutes, or until the chicken is cooked through. Drain thoroughly and transfer to a clean work surface. When the chicken is cool enough to handle, using 2 forks, shred the chicken. (Use one fork to hold the chicken steady on the cutting board. Use the other fork to tear the chicken into bite-sized pieces.)

4 Pickle the rhubarb

While the chicken cooks, in a small pot, combine the vinegar, sugar and 2 tablespoons of water. Heat the mixture to boiling on high. Remove from heat and pour over the rhubarb. Set aside. Rinse out the pot.

5 Finish & plate your dish

In a medium bowl, combine the mustard, poppy seeds and 2 tablespoons of the rhubarb pickling liquid. Slowly whisk in 2 tablespoons of olive oil until combined; season with salt and pepper to taste. In a large bowl, combine the shredded chicken, pickled rhubarb, smashed potatoes, cooked asparagus, chopped tarragon, radishes, crumbled goat cheese and poppy seed dressing. Season with salt and pepper to taste and toss to thoroughly coat. To plate your dish, divide the butter lettuce and hearty spring salad between 2 dishes.

Spring
Aromatics

FIELD GUIDE TO SPRING AROMATICS

The following are some of our favorite heirloom and specialty varieties. The best place to find them is at your local farmers' market, or you can grow them. The seeds are available at seed saver websites.

Chive Blossom: A springtime delicacy. The pastel-purple flowers of the chive plant. Has profusions of edible petals. Great eaten raw, or even fried. Has a mellow, garlicky taste.

Deep Purple Spring Onion: A kind of bunching onion (produces edible stalks rather than bulbs). Keeps its color when peeled. A vibrant addition to all kinds of dishes.

Noordhollandse Bloedrode Onion: A Dutch variety with a larger, above-ground "bulb." The name literally translates to "North Holland Blood Red."

Spring Leek: A version of the common leek harvested early, while still fairly small and thin. Has the same mild flavor as leeks, but with a more delicate texture. Cooking brings out a mellow sweetness.

Spring Onion: As the name implies, only available during spring. A variety of wild onion that has been eaten for thousands of years. Distinguished by its green shoots and small, almost spherical bulb.

White Spear Scallion: A bunching onion with vibrant, white, torpedo-like stalks. One of the most striking varieties. Easily distinguished by its bluish green leaves that taper down into white.

IN SPRING, A new kind of onion appears at farmers' markets. With its long, green stem and small, round bulb, the spring onion looks like a cross between a white globe onion and a scallion. And in fact, it's often confused with the latter: in America, they're both often called "green onions"; in Britain, they're both called "spring onions"; and in Australia, they're all called "shallots." But let's set the record straight, chefs: these are different vegetables.

While scallions grow straight upward (with a bulb that's almost flat) and shallots grow in elongated, garlic-like bunches, spring onions are simply young onions, harvested before they've had a chance to swell underground. That's why they were traditionally only available in spring:

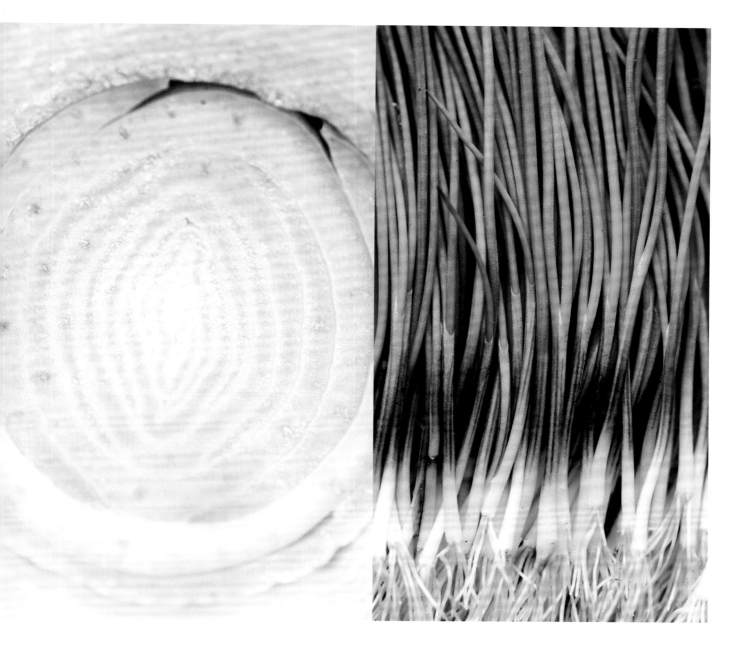

they have to be picked early, since later they lose their distinctive, light, fresh flavor. (Spring onions are actually so mild and sweet that they're eaten raw in salads.)

A similar, seasonal principle applies to a host of other vegetables. Garlic scapes are one of them. The green stalks of the flowering garlic plant, they're usually picked early by farmers and discarded, so that they can't divert any precious nutrients away from the bulbs. But, like the green tops of scallions (and even spring onions), these stems are a delicious ingredient. In flavor, they're like the rest of our favorite spring aromatics: delicate and complex—the perfect way to fill your kitchen with the scents of the season.

Chicken Piccata
with Garlic Scapes & Fresh Linguine Pasta

Garlic is essential to Italian cooking. Its flavors bring those of other traditional ingredients together. In springtime, though, we like to supplement garlic's powerful aromatic base with garlic scapes—the shoots of the garlic plant—for added delicacy and taste. Here, we add scapes to the pasta sauce and finish the linguine in them. It's our version of linguine "aglio e olio" (or with "garlic and oil") paired with chicken piccata. In this chicken preparation, pounded cutlets are sautéed and served with a savory sauce made with lemon, parsley and capers.

MAKES 2 SERVINGS • ABOUT 700 CALORIES PER SERVING

Ingredients

- 2 5-Ounce Chicken Cutlets, Pounded
- 3 Cloves Garlic
- 2 Ounces Garlic Scapes
- 1 Lemon
- 6-8 Sprigs Parsley
- 2 Tablespoons Capers
- 6 Ounces Fresh Linguine Pasta
- 3 Tablespoons All-Purpose Flour
- 2 Tablespoons Butter
- 3 Tablespoons Chicken Demi-Glace
- 2 Tablespoons Grated Parmesan Cheese

1 Prepare the ingredients & cook the pasta

Wash and dry the fresh produce. Heat a medium pot of salted water to boiling on high. Remove the chicken from the refrigerator to bring to room temperature. Peel and thinly slice the garlic. Slice the garlic scapes into 2-inch pieces. Using a peeler, remove the yellow rind of the lemon, avoiding the white pith; mince the rind to get 2 teaspoons of zest. Quarter the lemon and remove the seeds. Pick the parsley leaves off the stems; discard the stems. Roughly chop half the parsley leaves; keep the remaining leaves whole. Roughly chop the capers. Once the pot of water is boiling, add the pasta. Cook 3 to 5 minutes, or until al dente (slightly firm to the bite). Reserve ¾ cup of the pasta cooking water and drain the pasta thoroughly; rinse under cold water to prevent the noodles from sticking. Transfer to a large bowl and set aside in a warm place. Wipe out the pot.

2 Coat & cook the chicken

Place the flour on a plate. Season the chicken with salt and pepper on both sides. Coat both sides of the seasoned chicken in the flour (shaking off any excess). In a medium pan (nonstick, if you have one), melt half the butter on medium-high heat. Add the coated chicken and cook 2 to 3 minutes per side, or until golden brown and cooked through.

3 Make the piccata sauce

To the pan of cooked chicken, add the chicken demi-glace, capers, the juice of 2 lemon wedges, chopped parsley and ¼ cup of water. Cook, stirring occasionally, 2 to 3 minutes, or until the liquid has reduced slightly; season with salt and pepper to taste. Set aside in a warm place.

4 Make the pasta sauce

In the same pot used to cook the pasta, heat 2 teaspoons of olive oil on medium-high until hot. Add the garlic, garlic scapes and lemon zest; season with salt and pepper. Cook, stirring frequently, 2 to 4 minutes, or until the garlic is golden brown and the garlic scapes are bright green.

5 Finish the pasta & plate your dish

Add the cooked pasta, Parmesan cheese, remaining butter and ½ cup of the reserved pasta water to the pot of garlic and garlic scapes; season with salt and pepper. Cook, stirring frequently, 2 to 3 minutes, or until the pasta has absorbed some of the sauce. (If the sauce seems dry, add the remaining reserved pasta water until it reaches your desired consistency.) Remove from heat and season with salt and pepper to taste. Divide the finished pasta between 2 dishes and top each with a piece of the chicken piccata. Garnish with the whole parsley and remaining lemon wedges.

Lamb, Mint & Pea Orecchiette
with Purple Spring Onions

With a slightly mild flavor and a beautiful color, purple spring onions perfectly balance this dish's flavors. Lamb and mint have gone hand-in-hand throughout culinary history. We're using them together here to create a sauce for orecchiette, a small, ear-shaped pasta from Southern Italy. You'll finish the pasta in the sauce, soaking up the lamb's signature richness and the peppery bite of the mint.

MAKES 2 SERVINGS • ABOUT 700 CALORIES PER SERVING

Ingredients
8 Ounces Dried Orecchiette Pasta
6 Ounces English Peas, With Shells
3 Cloves Garlic
4 Sprigs Mint
1 Lemon
4 Ounces Purple Spring Onions
8 Ounces Ground Lamb
2 Tablespoons Butter
¼ Cup Grated Parmesan Cheese

1 Cook the pasta

Heat a medium pot of salted water to boiling on high. Add the pasta and cook 7 to 9 minutes, or until just shy of al dente (slightly firm to the bite). Reserve 1 cup of the pasta cooking water; drain the pasta thoroughly. Set aside.

2 Prepare the ingredients

While the pasta cooks, wash and dry the fresh produce. Shell the peas. Peel and thinly slice the garlic. Pick the mint leaves off the stems; discard the stems and finely chop the leaves. Using a peeler, remove the yellow rind of the lemon, avoiding the white pith; mince the rind to get 2 teaspoons of zest. Quarter the lemon and remove the seeds. Cut off and discard the root ends of the spring onions; thinly slice on an angle.

3 Cook the aromatics

In a large pan, heat 2 teaspoons of olive oil on medium until hot. Add the onions and garlic; season with salt and pepper. Cook, stirring frequently, 2 to 3 minutes, or until softened and fragrant.

4 Add the lamb

Using your hands, break the lamb into small pieces; add it to the pan of aromatics and increase the heat to medium-high. Season with salt and pepper and cook, stirring occasionally and breaking the meat apart with a spoon, 2 to 3 minutes, or until browned and cooked through.

5 Finish the pasta & plate your dish

Add the lemon zest, peas, cooked pasta, butter, the juice of 2 lemon wedges, half of both the Parmesan cheese and mint (save the rest for garnish) and ¾ cup of the reserved pasta water. Cook, stirring occasionally, 3 to 5 minutes, or until slightly reduced and thoroughly combined. (If the sauce looks dry, slowly add the remaining reserved pasta water until it achieves your desired consistency.) Remove from heat and season with salt and pepper to taste. Divide the finished pasta between 2 dishes and top with the remaining Parmesan cheese and mint. Garnish with the remaining lemon wedges.

Spring Root Vegetable Casserole
with English Peas, Spring Onions & Egg Noodles

In this recipe, we're using spring onions two ways to give this delicious vegetable casserole a special, seasonal bite. Treating them much like scallions, we're separating their white bottoms and green tops. The white bottoms are stronger and more sharply aromatic, so we're cooking them together with the rest of the filling. The white bottoms impart their flavor to the other ingredients, imbuing them with a savory, delicate, oniony taste. But the green tops are mild and beautiful, so we're sprinkling them over the cooked casserole as a garnish.

MAKES 2 SERVINGS • ABOUT 550 CALORIES PER SERVING

Ingredients

6 Ounces English Peas, With Shells
2 Cloves Garlic
2 Spring Onions
1 Bunch Lemon Thyme
1 Kohlrabi, Without Greens
1 Sweet Potato
5 Ounces Wide, Curly Egg Noodles
2 Tablespoons Butter
2 Tablespoons All-Purpose Flour
1 Cup Low-Fat Milk
½ Cup Grated Parmesan Cheese
¼ Cup Panko Breadcrumbs

1 Prepare the ingredients

Preheat the oven to 450°F. Wash and dry the fresh produce. Heat 2 medium pots of salted water to boiling on high. Shell the peas. Peel and mince the garlic. Remove and discard the root ends of the spring onions; thinly slice, separating the white bottoms and green tops. Pick the lemon thyme leaves off the stems; discard the stems and roughly chop the leaves. Peel and medium dice the kohlrabi and sweet potato.

2 Cook the vegetables

Once the first pot of water is boiling, add the kohlrabi and sweet potato. Cook 10 to 12 minutes, or until tender when pierced with a knife. Drain thoroughly and transfer to a bowl. Set aside.

3 Cook the noodles

While the vegetables cook and once the second pot of water is boiling, add the egg noodles. Cook 5 to 6 minutes, or until tender. Reserve 1 cup of the pasta water; drain the pasta thoroughly and set aside. Wipe out the pot.

4 Make the filling

While the vegetables continue to cook, in the same pot used to cook the noodles, melt the butter on medium heat. Add the flour, garlic and white bottoms of the spring onions; season with salt and pepper. Cook, stirring frequently, 1 to 2 minutes, or until the flour is golden and the onions are slightly softened. Stir in the milk and half the Parmesan cheese; season with salt and pepper. Cook, stirring frequently, 8 to 10 minutes, or until smooth and thickened. Remove from heat. Add the shelled peas, cooked vegetables, cooked noodles, ¾ cup of the reserved pasta water and all but a pinch of both the lemon thyme and the green parts of the spring onion (save the rest for garnish); mix to combine. (If the mixture seems too thick, add up to an additional ¼ cup of the reserved pasta water.)

5 Assemble & bake the casserole

Transfer the vegetable-pasta mixture to a medium baking dish. In a small bowl, combine the breadcrumbs and remaining Parmesan cheese; sprinkle evenly over the casserole. Bake the casserole 8 to 10 minutes, or until bubbly and browned. Remove from the oven and let stand for at least 5 minutes before serving. To plate your dish, divide the casserole between 2 plates and garnish with the remaining lemon thyme and green parts of the spring onions.

Triple Pork Mazeman
with Roasted Garlic & Snow Pea Tips

It seems almost impossible to exhaust the varieties of ramen. Mazeman is a very special version of the dish. Unlike most ramen soups, mazeman is "dry," meaning the noodles are coated in a thin sauce instead of a broth. This allows the toppings to take center stage. We're using spring vegetables, herbs and three kinds of pork (bacon, ground pork and a little pork demi-glace in the sauce). It's a light, refreshing take on the classic.

MAKES 2 SERVINGS · ABOUT 700 CALORIES PER SERVING

Ingredients
1 Head Garlic
1 Slice Bacon
2 Ounces Garlic Chives
2 Ounces Snow Pea Tips
1 1-Inch Piece Ginger
5 Ounces Ground Pork
2 Tablespoons Soy Sauce
2 Tablespoons Mirin
3 Tablespoons Pork Demi-Glace
12 Ounces Fresh Mazeman Noodles
¼ Teaspoon Black Sesame Seeds
¼ Teaspoon White Sesame Seeds
⅛ Teaspoon Kibbled Nori
⅛ Teaspoon Sansho Pepper

1 Roast the garlic

Preheat the oven to 475°F. Cut off and discard the top of the head of garlic (keeping the rest of the head as intact as possible). Place the garlic head on a piece of aluminum foil; drizzle with olive oil and season with salt and pepper. Tightly wrap the seasoned garlic in the foil and place on a sheet pan. Roast in the oven 28 to 30 minutes, or until very soft and lightly browned. Remove from the oven and carefully unwrap. Set aside to cool.

2 Prepare the ingredients

While the garlic roasts, wash and dry the fresh produce. Heat a large pot of salted water to boiling on high. Thinly slice the bacon. Mince the garlic chives. Cut the pea tips into 1-inch pieces. Peel and mince the ginger.

3 Cook the bacon & pork

In a medium pot, heat 1 teaspoon of olive oil on medium until hot. Add the bacon. Cook, stirring occasionally, 3 to 4 minutes, or until browned and crispy. To the pot of cooked bacon, add the ginger and all but a pinch of the garlic chives. Cook, stirring frequently, 2 to 3 minutes, or until softened and fragrant. Add the pork. Cook, frequently breaking apart the meat with a spoon, 4 to 5 minutes, or until cooked through; season with salt and pepper.

4 Make the sauce

While the pork cooks, and when the roasted garlic is cool enough to handle, using your hands, gently squeeze the roasted garlic cloves out of the head onto a clean work surface. To the pan of aromatics and pork, add the soy sauce, mirin, pork demi-glace, roasted garlic and 1 cup of water. Stir to thoroughly combine. Heat the sauce to boiling on high, then reduce the heat to medium and simmer, stirring occasionally, 2 to 3 minutes to develop the flavors.

5 Finish & plate your dish

Add the mazeman noodles to the boiling water. Cook, stirring occasionally, 3 minutes, or until tender. Thoroughly drain the noodles. Transfer directly to the pot of sauce. Cook, stirring constantly, 30 seconds to 1 minute, or until thoroughly combined. Remove from heat. Stir in the pea tips. Divide the pork ramen between 2 dishes. Garnish with the remaining garlic chives, the black and white sesame seeds, kibbled nori and sansho pepper.

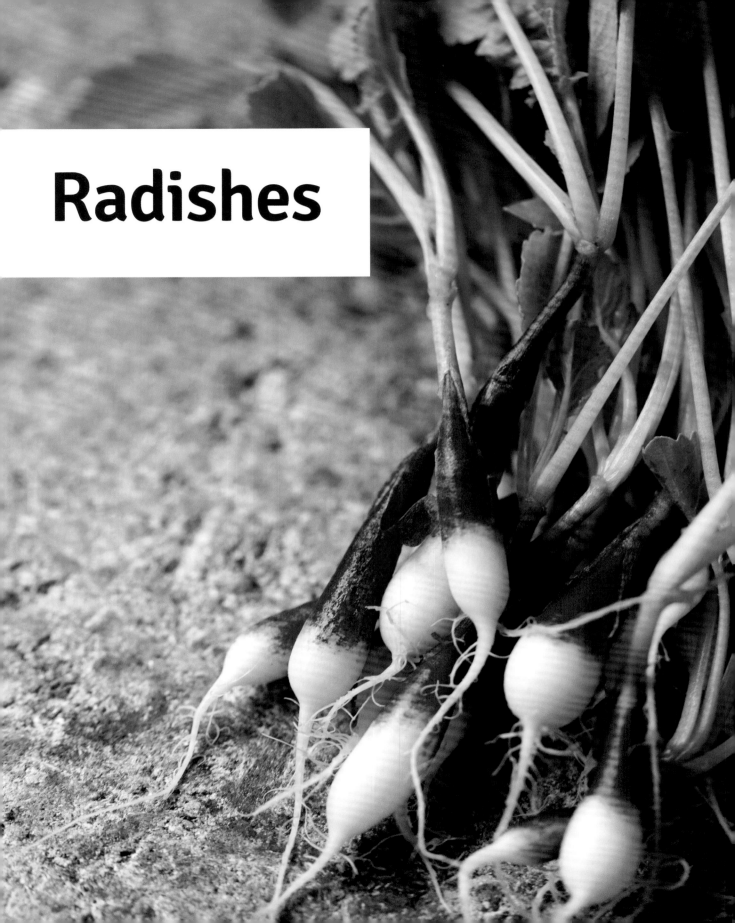

Radishes

FIELD GUIDE TO RADISHES

The following are some of our favorite heirloom and specialty varieties. The best place to find them is at your local farmers' market, or you can grow them. The seeds are available at seed saver websites.

Black Radish: A relative of the ancient wild radish. First cultivated in the eastern Mediterranean. One of the spicier varieties.

French Breakfast Radish: A milder-tasting, elongated variety. The tips are splashed with white. First introduced in France in 1879 and quickly became one of the most popular radishes in markets there.

Bora King Radish: A purple strain of daikon with delicious, tender leaves as well as an edible root. Slow to bolt, but gorgeous.

Purple Ninja Radish: A newer variety characterized by its purple skin and interior. Stripes running crosswise are said to resemble the masked eyes of ninjas slinking through lush gardens.

Cherry Bomb Radish: Spherical and bright red with a mildly spicy flavor.

Radish Sprouts: The tender shoots of the radish plant, harvested just after germination. Full of bright, peppery flavor and nutrients.

Chinese Green Luoba Radish: Incredibly popular in Northern Chinese cuisine. Resembles a daikon but with emerald-hued flesh.

Watermelon Radish: An heirloom daikon radish. Cross sections of the radish have a ring of green that surrounds a magenta center, resembling the cross section of a watermelon.

Daikon Radish: Native to Southeast and East Asia. Resembles a humongous white carrot. A key ingredient in traditional cuisines throughout Asia.

White Icicle Radish: A thin, cylindrical variety. Traders brought it to China in the 5th Century, where it was cultivated widely.

THE RADISH IS a root vegetable in the *brassica* (or cabbage) family. It is related to both the turnip and the horseradish—with which it shares smooth, tapered flesh and a sharp, peppery taste, respectively. It has been enjoyed around the world for thousands of years. In fact, it has long been ubiquitous in so many places that botanists have difficulty pinpointing its exact origins.

The Ancient Greek historian Herodotus described how those who built the Egyptian pyramids ate huge quantities of radishes, and bas-reliefs of radishes were likely carved on early pyramid walls. After the fall of the Roman Empire, radishes fell into relative obscurity. But they rose to prominence again in the British Isles around the time of Shakespeare—in

particular, because of their practicality as a winter root vegetable.

But gradually the winter radish became displaced by another variety: the spring radish. Imbued with a delicious, piquant flavor, which it shares with the mustard plant, the spring radish became a favorite of the English, who ate it raw with butter and salt. (As the 17th-Century herbalist John Evelyn remarked, radishes come with their own pepper.)

Now the dominant variety, spring radishes are an incredible way to add spiced kick to an array of dishes. Whether served raw and dressed, sautéed or roasted, they're unrivaled for their bright, sharp taste.

Chile-Dusted Fish Tacos
with Pickled Red Cabbage, Mango & Radishes

Spicy radish adds snap and crunch to this Mexican-inspired meal brimming with bright flavors and contrasting textures. Fresh cilantro and lime bring out the creaminess of the avocado and mango, while pickled red cabbage works in tandem with the radish to give a peppery kick to flaky, tender tilapia. The final product, assembled in traditional white corn tortillas, is as colorful as it is flavorful.

MAKES 2 SERVINGS • ABOUT 700 CALORIES PER SERVING

Ingredients

2 5-Ounce Tilapia Fillets
4 Ounces Radishes, Without Greens (About 4 Radishes)
1 Lime
1 Avocado
5-6 Sprigs Cilantro
1 Mango
¾ Pound Red Cabbage
¼ Cup Rice Vinegar
2 Tablespoons Mirin
1 Teaspoon Mexican Chile Powder
½ Cup All-Purpose Flour
8 6-Inch White Corn Tortillas

1 Prepare the ingredients

Wash and dry the fresh produce. Remove the fish from the refrigerator to bring to room temperature. Thinly slice the radishes into rounds. Quarter the lime. Pit, peel and large dice the avocado; season with salt and top with the juice of 1 lime wedge to prevent browning. Pick the cilantro leaves off the stems; discard the stems and roughly chop the leaves. Peel, pit and thinly slice the mango. Thinly slice the cabbage.

2 Pickle the cabbage

In a small bowl, combine the cabbage, rice vinegar and mirin; season with salt and pepper. Let stand to marinate, stirring occasionally to coat.

3 Cook the fish

Pat the fish fillets dry and season with salt and pepper on both sides. Coat with as much of the Mexican chile powder as you'd like (depending on how spicy you'd like the dish to be) then in the flour (shaking off the excess). In a large pan, heat a thin layer of olive oil on medium-high until hot. Add the fish; cook 2 to 3 minutes per side, or until golden brown and cooked through. Transfer to a paper towel-lined plate and set aside. Wipe out the pan.

4 Warm the tortillas & plate your dish

Working in batches, add the tortillas to the same pan used to cook the fish; heat on medium-high for 30 seconds to 1 minute per side, or until soft and pliable. Transfer to a plate and cover with a damp paper towel to keep warm. Make 4 tacos with 2 tortillas layered together for each. Divide the fish between the tacos. Top each with the avocado, radishes, pickled cabbage, mango and cilantro. Drizzle some of the pickled cabbage juices over each taco. Garnish with the remaining lime wedges.

Chicken Paillards
with Endive, Radishes & Haricots Verts

In this recipe, we're pairing spicy radishes with a
Belgian endive for a complex, delicious flavor profile.
Belgian endive is a prized vegetable not just because of
its smooth, crunchy leaves and uniquely tangy flavor,
but also because it's one of the most difficult vegetables
in the world to grow. The two-step process involves
nurturing the roots in a field, then growing the leaves in
a dark cellar. Combined with peppery radishes, the
endive gives these chicken paillards (a butterflied,
pounded chicken breast preparation) powerful, seasonal
flavor.

MAKES 2 SERVINGS • ABOUT 500 CALORIES PER SERVING

Ingredients
8 Ounces Fingerling Potatoes
5 Ounces Haricots Verts
4 Ounces Radishes, Without Greens (About 4 Radishes)
5-6 Sprigs Cilantro
1 Belgian Endive
1 Clove Garlic
1 Lime
2 5-Ounce Boneless, Skinless Chicken Breasts

1 Prepare the ingredients

Wash and dry the fresh produce. Heat a medium pot of salted water to boiling on high. Slice the potatoes into ¼-inch-thick rounds. Trim off the stems of the haricots verts. Trim and thinly slice the radishes. Roughly chop the cilantro stems and leaves. Cut off and discard the root end of the endive; separate the leaves. Peel and mince the garlic; smash with the side of your knife until it resembles a paste. Halve the lime.

2 Prepare the chicken

Lay the chicken breasts out on a clean, dry work surface. Carefully slice the chicken breasts horizontally toward the center (holding your knife parallel to the work surface), pulling the sliced meat back with your free hand as you go. (When the chicken breasts are fully butterflied, they should lie flat on the work surface like an open book.) Using the bottom of a pan or a flat meat mallet, evenly pound the chicken to a ¼-inch thickness.

3 Cook the haricots verts & potatoes

Fill a medium bowl with ice water; set aside. Add the haricots verts to the pot of boiling water. Cook 2 to 4 minutes, or until bright green and tender. Using a slotted spoon, transfer the haricots verts to the ice water, leaving the pot of water boiling on the stove. Add the potatoes to the pot of boiling water; cook 6 to 7 minutes, or until tender when pierced with a fork. Drain thoroughly and set aside.

4 Cook the chicken

While the potatoes cook, season the chicken with salt and pepper on both sides. In a large pan, heat 2 teaspoons of olive oil on medium-high until hot. Add the seasoned chicken and cook 2 to 4 minutes per side, or until browned and cooked through.

5 Dress the vegetables & plate your dish

In a small bowl, combine the garlic paste and the juice of one lime half; season with salt and pepper to taste. Slowly whisk in 2 tablespoons of olive oil until well combined. In a large bowl, combine the cooked haricot verts (draining before adding), cooked potatoes, radishes, endive and cilantro; season with salt and pepper. Add enough dressing to coat the vegetables (you may have extra dressing); toss to mix. Divide the chicken between 2 plates and top each with the dressed vegetables.

Seared Flat Iron Steaks
with Cherry Bomb Radishes, Snap Peas & Mashed Potatoes

Cherry bomb radishes are a delicious, crunchy variety with a mildly spicy kick. They're slightly sweet with a naturally earthy succulence, and they can really brighten up a sauté—like the one in this dish! We're cooking cherry bomb radishes with snap peas and garlic, and we're serving the sauté alongside rich, seared flat iron steaks. As a finishing touch, we're topping it all with a savory lemon-pepper sauce with tarragon and zest.

MAKES 2 SERVINGS • ABOUT 700 CALORIES PER SERVING

Ingredients

2 5-Ounce Flat Iron Steaks
¾ Pound Yukon Gold Potatoes
6 Ounces Sugar Snap Peas
4 Ounces Cherry Bomb Radishes, Without Greens (About 4 Radishes)
2 Cloves Garlic
1 Lemon
1 Shallot
3-4 Sprigs Tarragon
4 Tablespoons Butter
¼ Cup Heavy Cream
1 Teaspoon Coarsely Ground Black Pepper

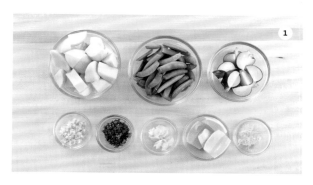

1 Prepare the ingredients

Wash and dry the fresh produce. Heat a medium pot of salted water to boiling on high. Remove the steaks from the refrigerator to bring to room temperature. Large dice the potatoes. Trim off and discard the ends of the snap peas. Cut the radishes into wedges. Peel and thinly slice the garlic. Using a peeler, remove the rind of the lemon, avoiding the pith; mince the rind to get 2 teaspoons of zest. Quarter the lemon and remove the seeds. Peel and mince the shallot. Pick the tarragon leaves off the stems; discard the stems and finely chop the leaves.

2 Cook the potatoes

Once the water is boiling, add the potatoes. Cook 14 to 16 minutes, or until tender when pierced with a fork. Drain thoroughly and return to the pot. Add 1 tablespoon of butter and as much of the heavy cream as you'd like. Using a fork, mash the potatoes. Season with salt and pepper to taste. Cover and set aside in a warm place.

3 Sauté the vegetables

While the potatoes cook, in a medium pan (nonstick, if you have one), heat 2 teaspoons of olive oil on medium-high until hot. Add the radishes and season with salt and pepper. Cook, stirring occasionally, 2 to 4 minutes, or until browned and slightly softened. Add the snap peas and garlic. Cook, stirring occasionally, 1 to 3 minutes, or until the snap peas are bright green and the garlic is lightly browned; season with salt and pepper to taste. Transfer to a plate and set aside in a warm place. Wipe out the pan.

4 Cook the steaks

While the potatoes continue to cook, season the steaks with salt and pepper on both sides. In the same pan used to cook the vegetables, heat 2 teaspoons of olive oil on medium-high until hot. Add the seasoned steaks and cook 3 to 5 minutes per side for medium rare, or until cooked to your desired degree of doneness. Transfer to a plate or cutting board to rest, leaving the browned bits (or fond) in the pan. Set aside in a warm place.

5 Make the lemon-pepper sauce & plate your dish

Add the shallot to the pan of reserved fond. Cook on medium heat, stirring frequently, 1 to 2 minutes, or until softened. Add the remaining butter, lemon zest, all but a pinch of the tarragon, the juice of all 4 lemon wedges, 2 tablespoons of water and as much of the black pepper as you'd like, depending on how spicy you'd like the dish to be. Cook, stirring frequently, 1 to 2 minutes, or until slightly reduced. Season with salt and pepper to taste; remove from heat. Find the lines of muscle (or grain) of the steak. Slice the steak crosswise, against the grain. Add any juices from the sliced steak to the vegetables; stir to combine. Divide the sliced steak, mashed potatoes and sautéed vegetables between 2 plates. Top each with some of the lemon-pepper sauce. Garnish with the remaining tarragon.

Almond-Crusted Cod
with Radishes, Fingerling Potatoes & Sautéed Kale

Roasting is a wonderful way to bring out the bright, tangy flavor of delicious spring radishes. The ambient heat of the oven cooks the radishes in their own juices, browning them on the outside and making them lightly crunchy and tender within. Potatoes, which are milder in taste, make a terrific pairing—the radishes add pop to the potatoes, and the potatoes mellow the radishes' piquancy. Together, they're the perfect side for cod fillets crusted in almond meal and cooked until flaky and golden.

MAKES 2 SERVINGS · ABOUT 620 CALORIES PER SERVING

Ingredients
2 Cod Fillets
6 Ounces Fingerling Potatoes
4 Ounces Radishes, Without Greens (About 4 Radishes)
2 Cloves Garlic
6 Ounces Green Kale
1 Lemon
3-4 Sprigs Parsley
1 Tablespoon Capers
3 Tablespoons Almond Meal
3 Tablespoons Butter

1 Prepare the ingredients

Preheat the oven to 450°F. Remove the fish from the refrigerator to bring to room temperature. Wash and dry the fresh produce. Cut the potatoes into 1-inch-thick rounds. Quarter the radishes. Peel and thinly slice the garlic. Remove and discard the kale stems; roughly chop the leaves. Using a peeler, remove the yellow rind of the lemon, avoiding the white pith; mince the rind to get 2 teaspoons of zest. Quarter the lemon and remove the seeds. Roughly chop the parsley leaves and stems. Roughly chop the capers.

2 Roast the radishes & potatoes

Place the radishes and potatoes on a sheet pan. Drizzle with olive oil and season with salt and pepper; toss to coat. Arrange in a single, even layer and roast 23 to 25 minutes, or until browned and tender when pierced with a knife.

3 Sauté the kale

Once the radishes and potatoes have roasted for about 10 minutes, in a small pan, heat 2 teaspoons of olive oil on medium until hot. Add the garlic and cook, stirring frequently, 30 seconds to 1 minute, or until fragrant. Add the kale, lemon zest and ¼ cup of water; season with salt and pepper. Cook, stirring occasionally, 5 to 7 minutes, or until wilted. Wipe out the pan.

4 Coat & cook the fish

While the vegetables continue to roast, place the almond meal on a plate. Season the cod fillets with salt and pepper on both sides. Press one side of each seasoned fillet into the almond meal to thoroughly coat (shaking off the excess). In the same pan used to cook the kale, heat 2 teaspoons of olive oil on medium-high until hot. Add the coated cod fillets and cook, crust side down first, 2 to 3 minutes per side, or until golden brown and cooked through. Transfer to a plate and set aside in a warm place.

5 Make the sauce & plate your dish

In a separate small pan, melt the butter on medium-high heat. Cook, stirring occasionally, 1 to 2 minutes, or until fragrant and deep golden brown. (The butter will bubble, then the foam will subside). Remove from heat and stir in the capers, the juice of all 4 lemon wedges and half the parsley; season with salt and pepper to taste. Divide the roasted vegetables and sautéed kale between 2 dishes. Top each with a cooked cod fillet and a few spoonfuls of the sauce. Garnish with the remaining parsley.

From the Kitchens of Our Home Chefs

Weekend Projects

The following two projects are designed to teach new culinary techniques—with delicious results. Let's celebrate the freshness of the season.

How to Make Perfect Pesto

In spring, as the land is reinvigorated, some of the first plants to come back into season are fresh herbs—green, full of life and incredibly flavorful. We're glad to have them back. And one of our favorite ways to celebrate them is to make fresh pesto! This sauce, which originated in Genoa, Italy, is simplicity itself. Pesto sauce typically doesn't need to be cooked, but rather relies on the freshness of its ingredients. The classic recipe for pesto includes only basil, garlic, pine nuts, salt and a hard cheese. The ingredients are traditionally mashed together using a mortar and pestle. In our version, we're taking tradition to the next level. You'll still use fresh herbs, but you'll be adding ramps (a special spring onion available only in—you guessed it—spring). And instead of pine nuts, you'll use toasted almonds as the base. Here, we're finely chopping the ingredients, but if you'd prefer, you can blend them in a food processor. Or you can get old school and use a mortar and pestle, if you have them. However you make it, this pesto is amazingly fresh and versatile. Use it on sandwiches and pizza, or in pasta sauces and vinaigrettes. It's best to either eat the pesto immediately after making it, or store it in the fridge topped with a thin layer of olive oil to prevent oxidation. Alternatively, you can freeze it in ice cube trays, keeping it on hand to use throughout the season. Finally, because of the simplicity of this recipe, using a high-quality olive oil is key to achieving the perfect flavor.

Ramp Pesto

MAKES 3 CUPS

Ingredients

2 Cloves Garlic
1 Large Bunch Parsley (About 8 Ounces)
1 Bunch Basil (About 1 Ounce)
1 Bunch Ramps (About 4 Ounces)
⅓ Cup Almonds, Raw & Skin-On
¾ Cup Grated Pecorino Cheese

Special Equipment

Food Processor (Optional)

1 **Prepare the ingredients**
Wash and dry the fresh produce. Peel and mince the garlic; smash with the side of your knife until it resembles a paste. Pick the parsley and basil leaves off the stems; discard the stems. Remove and discard the root ends of the ramps; cut into 1-inch pieces.

2 **Toast the nuts**
Heat a small pan on medium-high until hot. Add the almonds and toast, stirring frequently, 1 to 3 minutes, or until browned and fragrant. Transfer to a cutting board.

3 **Chop the ingredients**
When cool enough to handle, finely chop the toasted almonds. Add the parsley, basil and ramps and mince, occasionally mixing with your hands, until thoroughly combined. (Alternatively, blend the ingredients in a food processor with a little olive oil.) Transfer the mixture to a medium bowl.

4 **Finish the pesto**
Add the garlic paste and Pecorino cheese to the minced herbs and ramps. Slowly stir in enough olive oil to create a thick paste. Season with salt and pepper to taste.

PICK YOUR OWN PESTO ADVENTURE

Pesto has countless variations. Below, we're mixing it up and giving you four more of our favorites. Before making the fourth, you'll need to cook the beets. Boil them for 20 to 22 minutes, then rub off their skins with paper towels and your fingers. We also encourage you to experiment! Try substituting in your favorite herbs, nuts and hard cheeses.

	BASE	NUT	CHEESE
1	Ligurian Basil	Pine Nuts	Parmesan
2	Arugula	Pistachios	Pecorino Fioro Sardo
3	Fennel with Fronds	Walnuts	Piave
4	Beet + Tarragon	Sunflower Seeds	Garrotxa

Homemade Mozzarella

We're pushing freshness to the limit with this recipe. The only thing that can compare to the rich, buttery texture and mild flavor of fresh mozzarella is the texture and flavor of fresh mozzarella you've made yourself. And, as far as cheeses go, mozzarella is one of the easiest to make at home. This particular cheese is actually named for the process used to produce it. Traditionally, the milk is heated and allowed to separate into curds and whey. After it rests, the whey is drained off. The curds are then placed in hot water and pulled, stretched or spun. Next, the pieces are cut from the stretched cheese (the Italian word "mozzare" means "to cut"). Lastly, pieces are shaped into balls and either served immediately or stored in brine. The process, though straightforward, does require vigilance. Follow the directions carefully and get ready for fresh mozzarella like you've never had it before!

Homemade Mozzarella

After preparing your homemade mozzarella, you can
eat it immediately, or you can store it. If you're storing
it, place it in a water bath and keep it in the refrigerator,
changing the water daily. (Fresh mozzarella should be
eaten within two to three days.) Before you're ready to
serve it, take it out of the refrigerator to bring it to room
temperature, then season it simply with a drizzle of
high-quality olive oil, a sprinkling of salt and some
freshly-ground pepper.

MAKES 1½ POUNDS

Ingredients
¼ **Teaspoon Liquid Rennet**
1¼ **Cups Distilled Water**
1½ **Teaspoons Citric Acid**
1 **Gallon Whole Milk (Pasteurized, Not Ultra-Pasteurized)**
3 **Teaspoons Cheese Salt**

Special Equipment
Meat Thermometer
Fine Cheesecloth
Latex Gloves

1 Heat the milk & citric acid

Add the rennet to ¼ cup of cool distilled water; stir and set aside. In a separate bowl, mix the citric acid and 1 cup of cool distilled water until dissolved. In a large pot, combine the milk and citric acid mixture. Heat on medium-high, stirring occasionally to prevent scorching, until the thermometer reads 90°F.

2 Form the curds

Once the mixture reaches 90°F, slowly stir in the rennet mixture and continue to heat, slowly stirring with an up and down motion, but without breaking the surface, just to 110°F (no higher). Turn off the heat. Cover the pot and let stand, undisturbed, 30 minutes, to allow time for the curds to form. Once the curds are solid and shiny (and the curds and whey are clearly separated), using a knife, cut the curds into 1-inch cubes. Let stand for 5 more minutes to allow more whey to be released from the curds, to make the mozzarella firmer. Very gently stir the cubes for 1 minute and turn off the heat.

3 Strain the curds

Using a ladle, transfer the curds to a cheesecloth-lined strainer, leaving the whey in the pot. Set aside to drain for 10 to 15 minutes.

4 Prepare the water bath & warm the curds

While the curds drain, heat the reserved whey to 185°F and remove from heat. Using your hands, gently shape the curds into 4 equal portions and place on a plate; set aside. Working one at a time, form each portion of the curds into a loose ball and wrap in the cheesecloth. Dip the ball into the heated whey for 30 seconds to 1 minute, or until the curds reach 135°F at the core.

5 Stretch & season the cheese

Remove the curds from the cheesecloth and add as much of the cheese salt as you'd like. Using gloved hands, quickly mix in the salt by stretching and folding the cheese 8 to 10 times. The cheese should start to tighten and become firm; avoid overworking. (If necessary, dip the cheese into the heated whey again to reheat.) Eat immediately or store.

Feasts
with friends

The following, scaled-up recipes are designed to feed ten to twelve. These feasts are simple, seasonal and, most importantly, incredibly delicious.

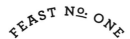

Roast Leg of Lamb

with Sautéed Artichokes
& Smashed New Potatoes

Though we may not think of meat as a "seasonal" ingredient today, that hasn't always been the case. Lamb is strongly associated with spring celebrations and feasts because, historically, it came to market only in the springtime. The lamb was regarded as a symbol of the new season and the new beginnings it brought. Today, lamb is available year-round, but we still love to participate in the tradition. The centerpiece of this delicious feast is a roasted leg of lamb, stuffed with herbs and aromatics. You'll also use seasonal vegetables to create two hearty sides to round out the spread. New potatoes (particularly popular in British Easter dinners) are picked before they're fully mature and are prized for their flavor. And what could be more "springtime" than artichokes? These delicious, earthy globes are at their best in this season. Spring has sprung; let's celebrate with friends!

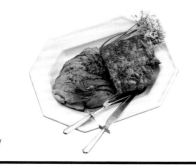

Roast the lamb | Prepare the artichokes | Cook the potatoes | Enjoy!

Roast Leg of Lamb

MAKES 10 TO 12 SERVINGS

Ingredients
1 6-8 Pound Boneless Leg of Lamb
1 Head Garlic
1 Large Bunch Rosemary
1 Large Bunch Thyme
1 Lemon

Special Equipment
Butcher's Twine
Instant-Read Thermometer

1 Prepare the ingredients
Preheat the oven to 400°F. Remove the lamb from the refrigerator. Peel and trim off the ends of the garlic cloves. Pick the rosemary and thyme off the stems; discard the stems. Using a peeler, remove the rind of the lemon, avoiding the white pith; mince the rind to get 1 tablespoon of zest. (Reserve the lemon for another use.)

2 Make the rub
Mince the garlic and rosemary on a cutting board. Add the thyme and lemon zest and continue to mince, mixing occasionally with your hands, until thoroughly combined. Transfer to a bowl.

3 Season the lamb
Place the lamb skin side up on a clean work surface. Drizzle with olive oil and season with salt and pepper on both sides. Using your hands, thoroughly rub both sides with the garlic-lemon-herb mixture.

4 Tie the lamb
Roll the lamb into an evenly-shaped roast. Using as much butcher's twine as necessary, tie the rolled lamb into a uniform shape to ensure even cooking. Transfer to a roasting pan, or a wire rack over a high-sided sheet pan. Let rest at room temperature for 30 minutes to marinate.

5 Roast the lamb
Roast the lamb for 80 to 100 minutes, or until browned and an instant-read thermometer reads 125°F. Remove from the oven.

6 Rest & serve the lamb
Let the lamb rest for at least 30 minutes, loosely covering with aluminum foil. Cut off and discard the twine. Thinly slice the lamb and transfer to a serving dish.

Sautéed Artichokes
with Toasted Breadcrumbs & Lemon Aioli

In this incredible side dish, you'll explore the exquisite tenderness of one of our favorite spring vegetables: the artichoke. You'll brown artichokes in a hot pan and dress them with a little lemon to bring out their nascent complexity. For textural contrast, you'll create your own breadcrumbs. To add the perfect amount of richness, you'll make a simple aioli. Let's celebrate the simplicity of spring.

MAKES 10 TO 12 SERVINGS

Ingredients
1 Large Bunch Parsley
¼ Cup Kalamata Olives
4 Cloves Garlic
3 Lemons
6 Pounds Baby Artichokes
2 Pounds Globe Artichokes (About 4)
½ Cup Mayonnaise
1 Small Loaf Ciabatta Bread

1 Prepare the ingredients

Preheat the oven to 400°F. Tear the bread into small pieces. Pick the parsley leaves off the stems; discard the stems. Using the side of your knife, smash the olives; remove and discard the pits, then roughly chop. Peel all 4 garlic cloves. Smash 2 cloves; mince the remaining cloves, then smash with the side of your knife until they resemble a paste. Quarter 2 lemons and remove the seeds; halve the remaining lemon.

2 Prepare the artichokes

Fill a large bowl with water and the juice of both lemon halves. Trim off and discard the tips of the baby artichoke stems. Trim off and discard 1 inch from the tops of the baby artichokes (to remove the sharp points). Peel off and discard the tough, outer leaves until you reach the tender, middle leaves. Using a paring knife, cut off and discard the outer skins of the stems. Halve the baby artichokes lengthwise and add to the bowl of lemon water. Repeat this process with the globe artichokes, then cut in half lengthwise and, using a spoon, scoop out and discard the inner, spiny chokes.

3 Make the lemon aioli & toast the bread

In a medium bowl, combine the garlic paste, mayonnaise and the juice of 4 lemon wedges; season with salt and pepper to taste. Arrange the bread pieces on a sheet pan. Drizzle with olive oil and season with salt and pepper; toss to coat. Arrange in a single, even layer and toast in the oven 6 to 8 minutes, or until golden brown.

4 Cook the artichokes & plate your dish

Drain and pat the artichokes very dry with paper towels. In a large pan, heat 1 tablespoon of olive oil on medium-high until hot. Add the smashed garlic cloves and cook, occasionally tilting the pan to submerge the cloves in oil, 1 to 2 minutes, or until golden brown. Remove and discard the cloves, leaving the oil in the pan. Add the artichokes to the pan of oil and cook, stirring occasionally, 8 to 10 minutes, or until browned. Add ½ cup of water and cook, stirring occasionally, 1 to 2 minutes, or until the water has evaporated. Turn off the heat and stir in the juice of the 4 remaining lemon wedges; season with salt and pepper to taste. Transfer the cooked artichokes to a serving plate. Garnish with the toasted bread pieces, parsley and olives. Serve with the lemon aioli on the side.

Smashed New Potatoes

with Dill & Lemon Crème Fraîche

MAKES 10 TO 12 SERVINGS

Ingredients
3 Pounds New Potatoes
4 Cloves Garlic
1 Lemon
1 Large Bunch Mint
1 Large Bunch Dill
8 Tablespoons Butter
½ Cup Crème Fraîche

1 Boil & smash the potatoes
Heat a large pot of salted water to boiling on high. Thoroughly rinse and scrub the potatoes. Once the pot of water is boiling, add the potatoes and cook 20 to 22 minutes, or until tender when pierced with a fork. Drain thoroughly and set aside. When cool enough to handle, carefully smash the boiled potatoes with a fork or the flat side of your knife.

2 Prepare the ingredients
While the potatoes cook, wash and dry the fresh produce. Peel and mince the garlic. Using the flat side of your knife, smash the garlic until it resembles a paste. Using a peeler, remove the yellow rind of the lemon, avoiding the white pith; mince the rind to get 2 teaspoons of zest. Quarter the lemon and remove the seeds. Pick the mint and dill leaves off the stems; discard the stems.

3 Cook the smashed potatoes
In a large pan, melt half of the butter on medium heat. Add half the smashed potatoes in a single layer. Cook 4 to 6 minutes on the first side, or until lightly browned. Carefully flip and add the remaining butter; season with salt and pepper. Cook, swirling the butter occasionally, 2 to 3 minutes, or until lightly browned. Add half the garlic paste; cook, stirring occasionally, 30 seconds to 1 minute, or until the garlic is fragrant and the smashed potatoes are golden brown. Transfer to a serving dish. Repeat this process with the remaining potatoes, butter and garlic paste.

4 Make the lemon crème fraîche & serve
In a medium bowl, combine the crème fraîche, lemon zest and the juice of 2 lemon wedges; season with salt and pepper to taste. Garnish the potatoes with the dill, mint and remaining lemon wedges. Serve with the lemon crème fraîche on the side.

Grilled Chickens

with Asparagus & Fava Bean Salad
& Morel Mushroom Farro

As the weather warms, let's spend a little time outside! To celebrate spring, we've created this feast designed for the grill. We're using chickens that have been "spatchcocked." That's a fancy term for a relatively simple thing. Spatchcocked chickens are whole chickens that have been split down the back and deboned. Without bones, they cook faster. You'll season the chickens with pesto. (Try using the pesto recipe from the Projects chapter on p. 114.) We've also devised a new method for grilling. You'll place the seasoned chickens between two racks, then tie the racks together. This added pressure makes sure the chickens are uniform in thickness, so they will grill evenly. It also makes flipping easier and exposes the maximum amount of skin to the heat, ensuring a golden-brown, crispy crust with a smoky flavor. To complete the meal, you'll make two sides: a hearty farro dish with peas and morel mushrooms and a salad using fava beans, asparagus and fresh mozzarella. (Try using the mozzarella recipe from the Projects chapter on p. 118.) These recipes combine to make a perfect feast that can be enjoyed indoors or out!

Grill the chickens | Make the morel mushroom farro | Make the asparagus & fava bean salad | Enjoy!

Grilled Chickens
with Ramp Pesto Salsa Verde

MAKES 10 TO 12 SERVINGS

Ingredients
3 3-Pound Spatchcocked Chickens
2 Shallots
¼ Cup Red Wine Vinegar
3 Cups Ramp Pesto (p. 116)

Special Equipment
2 Large Wire Racks
Kitchen Twine
Instant-Read Thermometer

1 **Marinate the shallots**
Preheat your grill for medium-heat cooking. Remove the chickens from the refrigerator to bring to room temperature. Peel and mince the shallots and place in a bowl with the vinegar.

2 **Season the chickens**
Pat the chickens dry and drizzle with olive oil. Generously season with salt and pepper on both sides. Using your hands, rub the seasoning into the chickens.

3 **Grill the chickens**
Place one of the wire racks on top of a sheet pan. Arrange the chickens, skin side up, in a single layer on the wire rack. Place the second wire rack on top and press down to flatten the chickens between them. (If desired, tie the two racks together with kitchen twine.) Place the wire racks and chicken onto the grill, skin side down first. Cook 12 to 15 minutes, or until browned. Carefully flip the chickens and cook 8 to 10 minutes, or until an instant-read thermometer inserted into the thickest part of breast, without touching bone, reads 165°F. Carefully remove from the grill.

4 **Rest the chickens**
When cool enough to handle, remove the chickens from the wire racks and place on a sheet pan or serving platter to rest for at least 10 minutes, loosely covering with aluminum foil to keep warm.

5 **Make the ramp pesto salsa verde**
While the chickens rest, in a medium bowl, combine the shallot-vinegar mixture and ramp pesto; season with salt and pepper to taste.

6 **Serve your dish**
Transfer the rested chickens to a serving platter. Carve one of the chickens. Top with some of the salsa verde. Serve the remaining salsa verde on the side.

Asparagus & Fava Bean Salad
with Fresh Mozzarella

MAKES 10 TO 12 SERVINGS

Ingredients
3 Pounds Fava Beans, In Shells
2 Lemons
2 Shallots
1 Pound Purple Asparagus
1 Pound Green Asparagus
1 Large Bunch Basil
1 Pound Fresh Mozzarella (p. 118)

1 Prepare the ingredients
Wash and dry the fresh produce. Heat a large pot of salted water to boiling on high. Shell the fava beans; discard the pods. Using a peeler, remove the rind of 1 lemon, avoiding the white pith; mince the rind to get 2 teaspoons of zest. Cut both lemons in half. Peel and mince the shallots. Trim off and discard the woody ends of the purple and green asparagus. Using a peeler, shave the purple asparagus into thin ribbons. Pick the basil leaves off the stems; discard the stems. In a medium bowl, combine the minced shallot and the juice of all 4 lemon halves.

2 Blanch the green asparagus
Fill a medium bowl with ice water. Add the green asparagus to the pot of boiling water. Cook 2 to 3 minutes, or until slightly tender and bright green. Using tongs, transfer to the bowl of ice water, leaving the boiling water in the pot. Let stand until cool, then drain again. Cut the cooled asparagus into 2-inch pieces on an angle. Set aside.

3 Blanch the fava beans
Fill a second medium bowl with ice water. Add the fava beans to the pot of boiling water used to blanch the green asparagus. Cook 3 to 4 minutes, or until tender. Drain thoroughly and transfer to the bowl of ice water. Let stand until cool, then drain again. Using your fingertips, break off the tips of the fava beans and squeeze the beans out of their outer skins; discard the skins. Set the prepared beans aside.

4 Make the dressing
Season the lemon-shallot mixture with salt and pepper to taste. Slowly whisk in ¼ cup of olive oil until thoroughly combined. Set aside.

5 Season the mozzarella
Tear the mozzarella into bite-sized pieces. Drizzle with olive oil and season with salt and pepper to taste; toss to coat. Transfer to a serving dish.

6 Finish & serve your dish
Just before serving, in a large bowl, combine the purple asparagus, green asparagus, fava beans, lemon zest, basil (tearing the leaves just before adding) and as much of the dressing as you'd like; season with salt and pepper to taste. Toss to coat. Transfer to the serving dish of seasoned mozzarella.

Morel Mushroom Farro

with English Peas & Walnut Dressing

MAKES 10 TO 12 SERVINGS

Ingredients

10 to 12 Fresh Morel Mushrooms
1 Shallot
1 Large Bunch Chervil
1 Bunch Thyme
2 Tablespoons Sherry Vinegar
2 Pounds English Peas, In Shells
3 Cups Pearled Farro
1 Tablespoon Butter
2 Tablespoons Walnut Oil

1 **Prepare the ingredients**
Wash and dry the fresh produce. Heat a large pot of salted water to boiling on high. Trim off and discard the ends of the morels; cut them in half lengthwise and quickly dip in water to clean. Peel and mince the shallot. Pick the chervil and thyme leaves off the stems; discard the stems. Place half the shallot in a bowl with the vinegar.

2 **Blanch the peas & cook the farro**
Fill a medium bowl with ice water; set aside. Add the peas to the pot of boiling water. Cook 30 seconds to 1 minute, or until bright green. Using a strainer, transfer to the bowl of ice water, leaving the boiling water in the pot. Let stand until cool, then drain again. Transfer to a large bowl; season with salt and pepper to taste. Add the farro to the pot of boiling water used to cook the peas. Cook 14 to 16 minutes, or until tender. Drain thoroughly. Transfer to the bowl of cooked peas.

3 **Cook the morel mushrooms**
While the farro cooks, in a large pan (nonstick, if you have one), heat 2 teaspoons of olive oil on medium-high until hot. Add the morels and season with salt and pepper. Cook, stirring occasionally, 2 to 3 minutes, or until crispy. Add the butter, thyme and remaining minced shallot. Cook, stirring occasionally, 30 seconds to 1 minute, or until softened and fragrant. Transfer to the bowl of cooked peas and farro; season with salt and pepper to taste.

4 **Make the dressing & serve your dish**
Season the shallot-vinegar mixture with salt and pepper to taste. Slowly whisk in the walnut oil and 2 tablespoons of olive oil until combined. Add as much of the dressing as you'd like to the cooked farro, peas and morels; toss to thoroughly combine. Transfer to a serving bowl. Garnish with the chervil.

Desserts

The dessert recipes in this chapter put a sweet, light spin on the season's unique produce.

144 Strawberry Layer Shortcake

146 Green Tea Crème Brûlée
148 Mascarpone Cheesecake

Rhubarb Crumble

A crumble is a type of pastry-like topping that became popular in the 20th Century. It's usually sprinkled over the top of a crust-less fruit pie. Unlike traditional pastry crusts, it's incredibly simple and quick to make. And yet, it's no less flavorful. Here, the walnut crumble is a wonderfully sweet textural element, providing the perfect counterpoint for the slightly tart rhubarb filling.

MAKES 10 TO 12 SERVINGS

Ingredients
1 Vanilla Bean
1¼ Cups Granulated Sugar
2 Pounds Rhubarb
¼ Teaspoon Dried, Ground Orange Peel
¼ Teaspoon Ground Cardamom
1½ Cups All-Purpose Flour
½ Cup Butter
1 Cup Walnuts, Shelled & Raw
1 Cup Light Brown Sugar

Special Equipment
Food Processor

1 Infuse the sugar
Preheat the oven to 425°F. Cut the vanilla bean in half lengthwise; using the flat side of a knife, scrape out and reserve the seeds. (Discard or save the pod for another use.) In a large bowl, combine the granulated sugar and vanilla bean seeds. Using your hands, massage the mixture together.

2 Make the rhubarb mixture
Wash and dry the rhubarb; trim off and discard both ends. Cut in half lengthwise, then large dice. In a large bowl, combine the diced rhubarb, dried orange peel, cardamom, vanilla-infused sugar, one-third of the flour and a large pinch of salt.

3 Melt the butter
In a small pot, melt the butter on medium heat. Set aside in a warm place.

4 Make the walnut crumble
In the bowl of a food processor, combine the walnuts, brown sugar, remaining flour and a small pinch of salt. Pulse until the walnuts are finely chopped. Drizzle in the melted butter. Using your hands, mix until thoroughly combined and the mixture resembles wet sand.

5 Assemble & bake the crumble
Fill a 12-inch circular baking dish with the rhubarb mixture. Top with the walnut crumble, lightly pressing the crumble onto the rhubarb mixture to create an even layer. Bake 30 minutes, or until bubbling and golden brown on top. Remove from the oven and let stand for 10 minutes.

Strawberry Layer Shortcake

Shortcake is a perfect springtime dessert. Named for its use of "shortening" (in this case, vegetable oil), the cake is known for its crumbly texture, which goes perfectly with sweet berries and whipped cream. Our tall version—four layers topped with a cluster of fresh strawberries and mint—is great both to have around as a sweet treat and to make for special occasions.

MAKES 10 TO 12 SERVINGS

Ingredients

1 Lemon
5-6 Sprigs Mint
2 Quarts Strawberries
1 Tablespoon Crème De Cassis
1¾ Cups Sugar
2¼ Cups Cake Flour
1 Tablespoon Baking Powder
5 Egg Yolks
1 Tablespoon Plus 1 Teaspoon Vanilla Extract
½ Cup Vegetable Oil
8 Egg Whites
½ Teaspoon Cream of Tartar
2 Cups Heavy Cream
6 Tablespoons Powdered Sugar

1 Prepare the ingredients

Preheat the oven to 325°F. Lightly grease two 9-inch cake pans; line each with parchment paper. Using a peeler, remove the rind of the lemon, avoiding the pith; mince the rind to get 2 teaspoons of zest. Quarter the lemon and remove the seeds. Pick the mint off the stems; discard the stems. Hull and thinly slice all but a few of the strawberries. In a large bowl, combine the sliced strawberries, crème de cassis, ¼ cup of granulated sugar and the juice of 2 lemon wedges. In a medium bowl, combine the cake flour, 1¼ cups of granulated sugar, the baking powder and 1 teaspoon of salt.

2 Make the batter

In separate large bowl, whisk the egg yolks, vegetable oil, lemon zest, 1 tablespoon of vanilla extract and ¾ cup of water until smooth. Add the egg yolk mixture to the flour mixture; stir until smooth. Rinse and wipe out the bowl. In the same bowl used for the egg yolk mixture, using a whisk, beat the egg whites and cream of tartar until soft peaks form. Add the remaining ¼ cup of granulated sugar and beat until the peaks are stiff. Using a spatula, fold one-quarter of the egg white mixture into the egg yolk mixture until smooth, then gently fold in the remaining egg whites.

3 Bake the cakes

Divide the batter between the prepared cake pans. Bake 35 to 45 minutes, or until a toothpick inserted into the middle comes out clean. Transfer the cakes to a wire rack and let cool completely. Run a knife around the edge of the pans; working one at a time, flip each cake onto a wire rack, then flip them again onto a cutting board.

4 Mash the fillings & assemble the cake

While the cakes bake, using a fork, mash about one-fourth of the sliced berries. Set aside. In a large bowl, combine the heavy cream, powdered sugar and 1 teaspoon of vanilla extract; beat until stiff peaks form. Using a long knife, carefully divide each cake layer in half horizontally to create four cake layers. Place 1 cake layer onto a serving platter and top with one-quarter of the whipped cream. Using a spatula, spread the whipped cream to the edge of the cake. Top with one-quarter of the strawberry mixture. Repeat with the remaining layers. Finish the cake by topping with the remaining whipped cream and remaining strawberries. Garnish with the mint leaves.

Green Tea Crème Brûlée

We're putting a gourmet spin on this French classic. Crème brûlée, or literally "burnt cream," is a custard dessert with a layer of crunchy caramel on top. In this recipe, we're infusing the custard with green tea to give it a delicate, nuanced flavor. The easiest way to caramelize the sugar for the crust is with a pastry torch. Keep a vigilant eye, as the caramel can burn easily—but watching the sugar transform is magical.

MAKES 8 SERVINGS

Ingredients
¾ Cup Granulated Sugar
8 Large Egg Yolks
4 Cups Heavy Cream
¼ Teaspoon Vanilla Bean Paste
2 Teaspoons Matcha Green Tea Powder
¼ Cup Turbinado Sugar

Special Equipment
8 6-Ounce Ramekins
Pastry Torch

1 Prepare the ingredients & heat the cream

Preheat the oven to 300°F. In a medium bowl, combine the granulated sugar and egg yolks; whisk until light yellow and thoroughly combined. In a medium pot, combine the heavy cream, vanilla paste, green tea powder and a big pinch of salt. Heat on medium 3 to 6 minutes, or just until small bubbles start to form around the edge of the pot. (Do not let boil.) Remove from heat.

2 Combine the egg yolk & heavy cream mixtures

Whisk a small amount of the heavy cream mixture into the egg yolk mixture until combined. (Called tempering, this process prevents the eggs from curdling.) Gradually whisk the remaining heavy cream mixture into the eggs. Strain the cream mixture through a fine-mesh strainer.

3 Bake the custards

Place eight 6-ounce ramekins onto one or more high-sided sheet pans. Using a ladle or a measuring cup, divide the egg yolk-heavy cream mixture between the ramekins. Place the sheet pans onto an oven rack; carefully add 1 inch of hot water around the sides of the ramekins to create a water bath. Loosely cover with aluminum foil. Bake 35 to 45 minutes, or until the custards are just set, but still slightly jiggly in the center. Let cool to room temperature or place in the refrigerator overnight.

4 Caramelize the sugar

Evenly top the cooled custards with the turbinado sugar. Using a pastry torch, carefully heat the sugar until it melts and forms a crispy top. Let stand for at least 5 minutes before serving.

Mascarpone Cheesecake

Though it's not a cake in the strictest sense of the word, cheesecake is still one of our favorites. It's technically a kind of tart, and, as far as desserts go, it's one of the most ancient. Recipes for distant ancestors of modern cheesecakes can be found the world over and date back as far as the 2nd Century. While we're not going that far back into history, this recipe is classic nonetheless. You'll make a mascarpone and lemon zest filling and pour it into a graham cracker crust to create a time-tested favorite.

MAKES 10 TO 12 SERVINGS

Ingredients

1 Lemon
12 Tablespoons Butter
10 Ounces Graham Crackers (About 18 Crackers)
¾ Cup Brown Sugar
16 Ounces Mascarpone Cheese, Softened
16 Ounces Cream Cheese, Softened
½ Cup Heavy Cream
1 Cup Granulated Sugar
4 Eggs
1 Tablespoon Vanilla Extract

Special Equipment
Springform Pan
Stand Mixer

1 Prepare the ingredients & make the crust

Position an oven rack in the center of the oven. Preheat the oven to 325°F. Using a peeler, remove the rind of the lemon, avoiding the pith; mince the rind to get 2 teaspoons of zest. Quarter and deseed the lemon. In a small saucepan, melt the butter on medium heat. In the bowl of a food processor, combine the graham crackers and brown sugar. Pulse until finely ground and thoroughly combined. Add the melted butter and a big pinch of salt. Pulse until the mixture resembles wet sand. Transfer to a 12-inch springform pan. Firmly press the mixture into the bottom and sides of the pan to create an even crust. Set aside.

2 Start the filling

In the bowl of a stand mixer fitted with the paddle attachment, combine the mascarpone cheese, cream cheese, heavy cream, granulated sugar and a big pinch of salt. Beat on medium-high speed for 3 to 4 minutes, or until thoroughly combined and creamy; scrape down the sides and bottom of the bowl.

3 Finish the filling

To the mascarpone-cream cheese mixture, beat in the eggs, one at a time, on medium-high speed for 30 seconds to 1 minute, or until thoroughly combined; scrape down the sides and bottom of the bowl. Add the vanilla, lemon zest and the juice of 3 lemon wedges. Mix on medium-high speed just until combined. Pour the finished filling into the pan with the crust.

4 Bake & serve the cheesecake

Transfer the assembled cheesecake to a sheet pan. Place the sheet pan in the oven and carefully add about 1 inch of water around the base of the springform pan to create a water bath. Bake for 3 hours, or until just set in the center. Remove the pan from the oven and let cool for 20 minutes. Run a paring knife around the edge, then let cool completely. Cover and chill overnight before serving.

About Blue Apron

Blue Apron makes incredible home cooking accessible by delivering original recipes and fresh ingredients to customers nationwide.

Chefs around the world wear blue aprons when learning to cook, and the blue apron has become a symbol of lifelong learning in cooking. Blue Apron encourages continuous learning by introducing members to new ingredients, flavors and cooking techniques with seasonally-inspired recipes that are always delicious, easy and fun to prepare.